UNSHAKABLE
LEADERSHIP

*Unorthodox Management and New
Out-of-the-Box Ways to Motivate*

Leonhart Laponnel

CONTENTS

Title: Unshakable Leadership:

Unorthodox Management and New Out-of-the-Box Ways to Motivate

CHAPTER 1: INTRODUCTION - SHIFTING THE LEADERSHIP PARADIGM

Why unorthodox leadership matters
The need for change in the modern world

As the world around us continues to evolve, so too must our understanding of leadership. Gone are the days when a one-size-fits-all approach to management was sufficient for ensuring success.

Today's rapidly changing business landscape demands that leaders adapt to new challenges, embrace unconventional wisdom, and think outside the box. In this introductory chapter, we'll explore the importance of unorthodox leadership and the pressing need for change in the modern world.

Why Unorthodox Leadership Matters

Unorthodox leadership is characterized by its departure from traditional, hierarchical structures and its emphasis on more collaborative, egalitarian, and innovative approaches to managing people. This new style of leadership is particularly well-suited to today's dynamic and interconnected world, where businesses must be agile and responsive in order to thrive.

There are several reasons why unorthodox leadership is increasingly relevant and valuable:

The Changing Nature of Work:
The ways in which we work have changed dramatically in recent years. The rise of remote work, flexible hours, and the gig economy has given rise to a more diverse and fluid workforce. Traditional leadership styles, which often prioritize rigid hierarchies and strict adherence to rules, are ill-equipped to manage this new reality. Unorthodox leadership, on the other hand, is more adaptive and capable of addressing the unique challenges posed by today's working environment.

The Power of Diversity:
Research has consistently shown that diverse teams outperform homogeneous ones. By embracing unorthodox leadership styles that prioritize inclusion, empathy, and collaboration,

organizations can tap into the full potential of their diverse talent pools. This leads to greater innovation, improved decision-making, and ultimately, better business outcomes.

Employee Engagement and Retention:
Today's workforce is increasingly motivated by more than just financial compensation. Employees want to feel a sense of purpose, autonomy, and belonging in their work. Unorthodox leadership styles, which often emphasize employee happiness and well-being, can help foster this sense of engagement and loyalty. In turn, this leads to reduced turnover and higher levels of productivity.

The Need for Innovation:
In an increasingly competitive global marketplace, organizations must be able to innovate and adapt to stay ahead of the curve. Unorthodox leadership fosters a culture of creativity, risk-taking, and continuous learning, which is essential for driving innovation and maintaining a competitive edge.

The Need for Change in the Modern World

The world is changing at an unprecedented pace. Technological advancements, shifting social norms, and the pressures of globalization have all contributed to a highly dynamic and uncertain environment. In order to succeed in this brave new world, organizations must be super agile, adaptable, and forward-thinking. This necessitates a departure from traditional leadership models, which are often rigid, hierarchical, and resistant to change.

The following factors underscore the urgent need for a shift in the leadership paradigm:

The Rise of AI and Automation:
Artificial intelligence and automation technologies are poised to transform the world of work. Many routine tasks are being automated, necessitating a shift towards more complex, creative, and collaborative roles. Unorthodox leadership is well-equipped to manage this transition, as it prioritizes human skills such as empathy, adaptability, and critical thinking.

The Emergence of the Millennial Workforce:
Millennials now make up the largest generation in the workforce, bringing with them new expectations and values. This generation is characterized by a strong desire for work-life balance, personal growth, and social responsibility. Unorthodox leadership styles, which emphasize employee well-being and personal development, are better suited to meeting these needs.

The Growing Importance of Social and Environmental Responsibility:
Modern consumers and employees increasingly expect organizations to prioritize social

and environmental responsibility. Unorthodox leadership styles, which often emphasize values-driven decision-making and ethical considerations, are more aligned with these evolving expectations. By adopting unorthodox leadership practices, organizations can demonstrate their commitment to creating positive social and environmental impact, which in turn can enhance their reputation and strengthen their relationships with stakeholders.

The Impact of Globalization:
As the world becomes more interconnected, organizations must navigate a complex landscape of cultural, political, and economic factors. Traditional leadership styles, which (unfortunately still) often prioritize uniformity and control, may struggle to adapt to these diverse and dynamic contexts.
Unorthodox leadership, on the other hand, embraces flexibility, collaboration, and cross-cultural understanding, making it better equipped to manage the challenges of globalization.

The Increasing Pace of Change:
The rapid pace of change, driven by technological advancements and shifting market dynamics, has made adaptability and resilience more important than ever. Organizations that cling to outdated leadership models will most surely be left behind in the dust, while those that embrace unorthodox approaches are better positioned to navigate

uncertainty and seize new opportunities.

In light of these factors, it's clear that a shift in the leadership paradigm is not only desirable but necessary. The unorthodox leadership styles and strategies you will see in this book provide you with a roadmap to break free from convention and chart a new path toward success.

As you read through the chapters that follow, you'll discover a wealth of innovative ideas, tools, and techniques for reimagining leadership in the modern world. From the inverted management pyramid to hands-off leadership, happiness leadership, and beyond, each concept challenges traditional assumptions and offers fresh perspectives on what it means to lead in today's complex and rapidly evolving environment.

Throughout the book, we'll also share examples and tips to help you implement these unorthodox leadership practices in your own organization. By doing so, you'll not only cultivate a more engaged, creative, and resilient workforce but also foster a culture that embraces change, innovation, and continuous growth.

The tone of this book is conversational, approachable, and supportive, as though you're sitting down with a trusted executive coach who knows how to make the journey fun and enjoyable. Our goal is to inspire and empower you to explore new ways of leading, challenge the status quo, and ultimately, become the kind of leader that others admire and want to follow.

Some of the Unorthodox Leadership ideas may make you stop and think "Ahh- this is a bit too much for my organization". But we encourage you to keep an open mind, trust your intuition, and embrace the spirit of experimentation. After all, the most effective leaders are those who are willing to take risks, learn from their mistakes, and continually evolve in response to the world around them.

With each chapter, you'll gain new insights, perspectives, and strategies to help you navigate the challenges of the modern world and emerge as a more confident, resilient, and unorthodox leader. The path ahead may be unconventional, but as you'll soon discover, the rewards of embracing unshakable leadership are well worth the journey.

CHAPTER 2: HANDS-OFF LEADERSHIP

The philosophy behind hands-off leadership
Benefits and challenges of a hands-off approach

The traditional top-down, command-and-control leadership style is increasingly being challenged, and hands-off leadership emerges as a powerful alternative. This approach to leadership is characterized by a focus on empowering employees, providing them with the tools, resources, autonomy, and trust they need to succeed, and stepping back to allow them to make decisions and take ownership of their work. In this chapter, we'll explore the philosophy behind hands-off leadership, as well as the benefits and challenges that come with adopting this approach.

The Philosophy Behind Hands-off Leadership

At its core, hands-off leadership is about believing in the capabilities of your team and giving them the space and support they need to achieve their goals. This leadership style is grounded in several key principles, which together form the foundation of a hands-off approach to management:

Trust:
Hands-off leaders have faith in their employees' abilities and trust them to make the right decisions. By demonstrating confidence in their team, hands-off leaders foster a sense of trust and mutual respect that encourages employees to take ownership of their work and strive for excellence.

Autonomy:
Hands-off leadership prioritizes giving employees the freedom to make their own choices and determine their own paths to success. This sense of autonomy not only boosts employee engagement and satisfaction but also encourages innovation and creativity. The people in the trenches most often know how to do things in the most effective way.

Support:
While hands-off leaders may not be involved in every decision or task, they are always available to provide guidance, resources, and encouragement when needed. This support helps employees feel confident in their abilities and ensures they have

the tools they need to succeed.

Flexibility:
Hands-off leaders recognize that there is no one-size-fits-all solution to management and are willing to adapt their leadership style to the unique needs and preferences of their team. This flexibility allows employees to work in ways that are most effective and enjoyable for them, ultimately leading to greater productivity and job satisfaction.

Focus on Results:
Rather than micromanaging the details of how work is done, hands-off leaders concentrate on the outcomes. By setting clear expectations and holding employees accountable for results, hands-off leaders encourage a performance-driven culture that values achievement over rigid adherence to processes.

Benefits of a Hands-off Approach

There are numerous benefits to adopting a hands-off leadership style, both for the individual leader and the organization as a whole. Some of the key advantages of this approach include:

Empowered Employees:
When employees feel trusted and empowered, they are more likely to take initiative, think creatively, and be proactive in their work. This sense of empowerment can lead to higher levels of

job satisfaction, increased motivation, and greater commitment to the organization.

Innovation and Creativity:
By giving employees the autonomy to experiment, make decisions, and take risks, hands-off leaders create an environment that fosters innovation and creativity. This can help organizations stay ahead of the competition, adapt to changing market conditions, and capitalize on new opportunities.

Improved Decision-Making:
Research has shown that decentralized decision-making can lead to better, more informed decisions. When employees are given the freedom to make choices and contribute their ideas, organizations can tap into a diverse range of perspectives and expertise, ultimately leading to more effective problem-solving and decision-making.

Greater Agility and Adaptability:
When conditions change as rapidly as they do now; organizations must be agile and adaptable in order to survive and thrive. Market conditions we thought would last, can now change in a matter of days. Hands-off leadership encourages a flexible, responsive approach to work, making it easier for organizations to pivot in response to new challenges and opportunities.

Stronger Talent Retention:
A hands-off leadership style that emphasizes

trust, autonomy, and support can help attract and retain top talent. Employees who feel valued and respected are more likely to stay with an organization and contribute to its long-term success.

Challenges of a Hands-off Approach

While there are numerous benefits to hands-off leadership, it's important to acknowledge that this approach also comes with its own set of challenges. Successfully implementing a hands-off leadership style requires careful consideration and effort to navigate these potential obstacles:

Striking the Right Balance:
One of the main challenges of hands-off leadership is finding the right balance between giving employees autonomy and providing necessary guidance and support. Leaders must avoid the pitfalls of becoming too detached or disengaged, as this can lead to a lack of direction and support for the team. On the other hand, leaders should also be cautious not to slip back into micromanagement, which can undermine the very trust and autonomy they are trying to foster.

Accountability and Performance Management:
With a focus on results rather than processes, hands-off leaders must establish clear performance expectations and maintain a consistent system for tracking and evaluating

employee performance. You need to say, "You are free to navigate and make decisions – inside this framework". This can be really challenging for many leaders, as it requires leaders to resist the temptation to intervene in day-to-day tasks and instead, focus on coaching and mentoring employees to achieve desired outcomes.

Navigating Resistance to Change:
Adopting a hands-off leadership approach may be met with resistance from employees who are accustomed to more traditional, hierarchical management styles. In such cases, leaders must be prepared to communicate the benefits of this new approach and provide the necessary support and resources to help employees adapt to this change.

Building Trust:
For hands-off leadership to be successful, a strong foundation of trust must be established between leaders and their teams. This requires time, patience, and consistent demonstration of trustworthiness on the part of the leader. Building trust can be particularly challenging in situations where trust has been previously eroded or where a leader is new to the organization.

Adapting to Different Personalities and Work Styles:
Hands-off leadership requires leaders to be flexible and adaptable in their approach to managing different personalities and work styles. This can be

challenging, as it may require leaders to step way outside their comfort zones and develop new skills and strategies for connecting with and supporting their employees.

Despite these challenges, hands-off leadership offers a powerful and effective alternative to traditional management styles. By embracing the principles of trust, autonomy, support, flexibility, and a focus on results, leaders can empower their teams to achieve greater levels of success and satisfaction in the modern workplace.

As you consider implementing a hands-off leadership approach in your organization, keep in mind that change takes time and patience. It's essential to communicate the rationale behind this shift, provide ongoing support and resources, and remain open to feedback and adjustment as needed.

CHAPTER 3: INVERTED MANAGEMENT PYRAMID

Understanding the inverted pyramid
Empowering employees and encouraging collaboration

Traditional management structures often resemble a pyramid, with a single leader or a small group of executives at the top, middle managers in the center, and employees at the wide base. While this hierarchical approach has been the norm for many years, it is increasingly being challenged by more innovative and empowering organizational structures.

One such alternative is the inverted management pyramid, which flips the traditional hierarchy on its head and places employees at the top, with leaders and managers serving as support. In this chapter, we'll explore the concept of the inverted pyramid, its benefits, and how it empowers employees and encourages collaboration.

Understanding the Inverted Pyramid

The inverted management pyramid is a model that reimagines the roles and responsibilities of leaders, managers, and employees within an organization. In this structure, employees are positioned at the top of the pyramid, reflecting their central importance to the organization's success. Managers and leaders, on the other hand, occupy the lower tiers, with their primary role being to support and enable the success of their teams.

The inverted pyramid is grounded in the belief that the key to organizational success lies in empowering employees, giving them all the resources and support they need to excel in their roles, and fostering a culture of collaboration and shared decision-making. This approach stands in stark contrast to traditional top-down management structures, which often prioritize control and adherence to authority.

Empowering Employees and Encouraging Collaboration

The inverted management pyramid offers numerous benefits to organizations, particularly in terms of employee empowerment and collaboration. By placing employees at the top of the pyramid and focusing on their needs and success, organizations can create a more engaged, motivated, and productive workforce.

When you stop and think of it - It's really kind of logic. The employees most of the time know much better how to do their job. Receiving "orders" from above many times slows things down – and takes away the motivation. The managers need to put up the frame and the strategies – so everyone goes in the same direction.

Some of the key ways in which the inverted pyramid supports employee empowerment and collaboration include:

Shifting the Focus to Employee Needs:
In the inverted pyramid, the primary role of leaders and managers is to support and enable the success of their employees. This means actively listening to their concerns, providing resources and training, removing obstacles, and offering guidance when needed. By prioritizing employee needs, organizations can foster a culture of empowerment and engagement.

Encouraging Shared Decision-Making:
The inverted pyramid emphasizes the importance of including employees in decision-making processes, recognizing that their insights and perspectives are invaluable to the organization's

success. By involving employees in decisions that directly impact their work, organizations can foster a sense of ownership and commitment, while also benefiting from a diverse range of ideas and expertise.

Promoting Collaboration and Teamwork:

The inverted pyramid encourages collaboration and teamwork by breaking down hierarchical barriers and fostering a sense of equality among employees, managers, and leaders. This can lead to improved communication, increased trust, and more effective problem-solving and decision-making.

Supporting Professional Growth and Development:

In the inverted pyramid, managers and leaders are tasked with helping employees grow and develop in their roles. This includes providing regular feedback, coaching, and opportunities for professional development. By investing in employee growth, organizations can ensure they have a talented, skilled workforce that is well-equipped to drive success.

Fostering a Culture of Innovation:

By empowering employees and encouraging collaboration, the inverted pyramid creates an environment that is ripe for innovation. When employees feel supported, valued, and included, they are more likely to take risks, experiment with new ideas, and push the boundaries of what is possible.

Implementing the Inverted Management Pyramid

Successfully implementing the inverted management pyramid requires a shift in mindset and a commitment to embracing new ways of leading and managing. Here are some strategies to help you begin the process of adopting this empowering and collaborative approach to management:

Assess Your Current Management Structure:
Before implementing any changes, take the time to evaluate your organization's current management structure and identify areas where it may be overly hierarchical or restrictive.

Communicate the Vision:
Share your vision for adopting the inverted management pyramid with your team, explaining the benefits and the rationale behind the change. Open communication is crucial to ensure buy-in from employees, managers, and leaders alike.

Empower Employees:
Begin the process of empowering employees by involving them in decision-making, encouraging their input and ideas, and actively seeking their feedback. Ensure that employees have the

resources, training, and support they need to excel in their roles.

Rethink Managerial Roles:
Encourage managers to adopt a more supportive and facilitative approach, focusing on coaching, mentoring, and removing obstacles for their teams. This may require redefining performance metrics and expectations for managers to align with the goals of the inverted pyramid.

Foster Collaboration:
Break down silos and promote cross-functional collaboration within your organization. Encourage teamwork, open communication, and the sharing of ideas and expertise among employees, managers, and leaders.

Evaluate and Adjust:
As you implement the inverted management pyramid, regularly assess its impact on employee engagement, collaboration, and overall organizational performance. Be prepared to make adjustments and refine your approach as needed.

By implementing the principles of the inverted management pyramid, you can create a much more empowered, collaborative, and innovative workforce. This approach to management aligns well with other unorthodox leadership styles discussed throughout this book, offering a comprehensive framework for reimagining leadership in the modern world.

Always remember that the journey to unshakable leadership is one of continuous learning, growth, and evolution. By remaining open to new ideas, challenging the status quo, and trusting in the capabilities of your team, you'll be well on your way to becoming the kind of leader that others admire and want to follow.

CHAPTER 4: HAPPINESS LEADERSHIP

Prioritizing employee happiness
Creating a positive work environment

Companies are constantly looking for ways to stay ahead of the competition and market development. They are constantly seeking new ways to increase productivity, drive innovation, and stay ahead of the curve. While many leaders focus on strategies like improving efficiency, streamlining processes, and investing in cutting-edge technology, there is another, often overlooked, factor that can have a profound impact on an organization's success: **happiness.**

Happiness leadership is an approach that prioritizes employee well-being and satisfaction, recognizing that a happy workforce is a more engaged, motivated, and productive one.

In this chapter, we'll delve into the concept

of happiness leadership, explore the importance of prioritizing employee happiness, and provide practical strategies for creating a positive work environment.

Prioritizing Employee Happiness

Happiness leadership is grounded in the belief that employee happiness is a key driver of organizational success. Numerous studies have demonstrated that happy employees are more engaged, more productive, and more likely to stay with their organization than their unhappy counterparts. Furthermore, happiness has been linked to increased creativity, improved problem-solving abilities, and better decision-making. In short, happiness is good for both individuals and organizations.

By prioritizing employee happiness, leaders can create a virtuous cycle in which happy employees contribute to a positive, thriving work environment, which in turn, leads to even greater levels of happiness and success. Some of the key benefits of prioritizing employee happiness include:

Increased Employee Engagement:
When employees are happy, they are more likely to be engaged in their work and feel a strong sense of commitment to their organization. Engaged employees are more motivated, more willing to go

the extra mile, and more likely to contribute to the success of the organization.

Improved Productivity:
Research has shown that happy employees are more productive than their unhappy counterparts. When employees feel good about their work and their work environment, they are more focused, more efficient, and more likely to produce high-quality results.

Reduced Turnover:
Happy employees are more likely to stay with their organization, which means reduced turnover and associated costs. By prioritizing employee happiness, leaders can create a stable, loyal workforce that is committed to the organization's long-term success.

Enhanced Creativity and Innovation:
Happiness has been linked to increased creativity and innovation, as happy employees are more likely to think outside the box, take risks, and explore new ideas. By fostering a culture of happiness, leaders can create an environment that supports and nurtures innovation, helping their organization stay ahead of the competition.

Improved Teamwork and Collaboration:
Happy employees are more likely to work well with others, contributing to a positive, collaborative work environment. When employees feel good about their work and their colleagues,

they are more likely to share ideas, support one another, and work together towards common goals.

Creating a Positive Work Environment

So, how can leaders create a work environment that fosters happiness, well-being, and satisfaction? Here are some practical strategies for incorporating happiness leadership into your organization:

Foster a Culture of Trust and Respect:
A key component of employee happiness is feeling valued, trusted, and respected. Leaders can foster this sense of trust and respect by being transparent, honest, and open in their communication, actively listening to employee concerns and ideas, and demonstrating empathy and understanding.

Offer Flexibility and Autonomy:
Employees who have the freedom to make their own decisions and choose their own work styles are often happier and more satisfied in their roles. Leaders can support employee happiness by offering flexible work arrangements, allowing employees to take ownership of their work, and encouraging them to find their own paths to success.

Invest in Employee Growth and Development:
Employees who feel supported in their personal and professional growth are more likely to be happy in their jobs. Leaders can invest in employee happiness by offering ongoing training, mentoring, and development opportunities, as well as providing regular feedback and coaching to help employees reach their full potential.

Recognize and Reward Success:
One of the most powerful ways to boost employee happiness is by recognizing and rewarding their achievements. Leaders should make it a priority to celebrate individual and team successes, whether through formal recognition programs, informal praise, or tangible rewards. And remember that attention and recognition are often much more important – at least long term – than money.

Encourage Work-Life Balance:
While work is an important part of most people's lives, it's crucial for employees to maintain a healthy balance between their professional and personal lives. Leaders can promote work-life balance by respecting employees' personal time, encouraging them to take breaks and vacations, and modeling healthy work habits themselves.

Provide a Supportive and Inclusive Work Environment:
Employees are more likely to be happy in their jobs when they feel supported and included.

Leaders can foster a positive work environment by promoting diversity and inclusion, addressing any issues of discrimination or harassment, and ensuring that all employees feel valued and respected.

Foster Open Communication:
Open and honest communication is a cornerstone of a positive work environment. Encourage employees to share their ideas, concerns, and feedback, and make sure to listen actively and respond thoughtfully. This will not only boost employee happiness but also contribute to a more collaborative and innovative workplace.

Prioritize Health and Wellness:
A healthy workforce is a happy workforce. Invest in employee well-being by offering wellness programs, providing access to resources and support for mental and physical health, and creating a safe, comfortable work environment.

By incorporating these strategies into your leadership approach, you can create a work environment that promotes happiness, well-being, and satisfaction. As you continue to prioritize employee happiness and embrace happiness leadership, you'll likely see the benefits ripple throughout your organization, from increased productivity and innovation to improved teamwork and collaboration.

Happiness leadership is an unorthodox but

powerful approach to leading and managing. By prioritizing employee happiness and creating a positive work environment, leaders can unlock the full potential of their workforce and drive their organization towards greater levels of success.

Remember, a happy workforce is a productive, innovative, and loyal one, and as a leader, your role in fostering happiness is critical to your organization's long-term success.

CHAPTER 5: SERVANT LEADERSHIP

Putting employees first
How to be a servant leader

This concept might have many traditional managers throw away this book in disgust. But keep an open mind. You won't be running around in white knee pants like at an ancient king's court serving your employees coffee and biscuits all day long.

Servant leadership is a unique approach to leadership that emphasizes putting the needs of employees first, in order to create an environment where they can thrive, grow, and excel in their roles. As you see many of the concepts, we touch on in this book are quite similar – but they have some important differences also.

But take what you like from each of them – and make your own unorthodox leadership cocktail.

Mix and match the leadership style that benefits you and your employees the best.

Servant leaders understand that by focusing on the well-being and development of their team members, they are ultimately fostering a more engaged, motivated, and high-performing workforce. In this chapter, we'll explore the concept of servant leadership, its core principles, and practical strategies for becoming a servant leader who puts employees first.

Understanding Servant Leadership

The term "servant leadership" was first coined by Robert K. Greenleaf in his 1970 essay "The Servant as Leader." Greenleaf believed that the most effective leaders were those who prioritized the needs and well-being of their employees over their own self-interests. He argued that by focusing on the growth and development of their team members, leaders would naturally create an environment where employees felt valued, empowered, and motivated to contribute to the organization's success.

Servant leadership is a values-based leadership approach, grounded in the belief that the primary responsibility of a leader is to serve others. Unlike traditional leadership models that prioritize power, control, and authority, servant leadership emphasizes empathy, humility, and a genuine concern for the well-being of others. By putting employees first and ensuring their needs are met, servant leaders create a culture where individuals feel valued, supported, and inspired to do their best work.

Core Principles of Servant Leadership

Servant leadership is guided by a set of core principles that shape the way leaders interact with and support their employees. These principles include:

Empathy:
Servant leaders genuinely care about the well-being and success of their employees. They strive to understand their team members' needs, feelings, and perspectives, and take these into consideration when making decisions.

Humility:
Servant leaders recognize that they are not the sole source of wisdom, knowledge, or expertise within their organization. They value the contributions of others and are willing to listen, learn, and adapt.

Stewardship:
Servant leaders view themselves as stewards of their organization's resources, including its human capital. They are committed to ensuring that employees have the support, tools, and opportunities they need to grow and succeed in their roles.

Commitment to the Growth of Others:
Servant leaders prioritize the personal and professional development of their employees. They invest in training, mentoring, and coaching to help their team members unlock their full potential.

Building Community:
Servant leaders understand the importance of fostering a sense of belonging and community within their organization. They work to create an inclusive, supportive environment where employees feel connected to one another and to the organization's mission and values.

How to Be a Servant Leader

Becoming a servant leader requires quite a big shift in mindset for many leaders, as well as the development of specific skills and behaviors. Here are some practical strategies for embracing servant leadership and putting employees first:

Actively Listen:
One of the most important skills a servant leader can develop is the ability to listen actively and empathetically to their employees. This means not only hearing what is being said but also seeking to understand the underlying emotions, needs, and concerns. By cultivating this skill, you'll be better equipped to support your team members and make informed decisions that take their

perspectives into account.

Foster a Collaborative Environment:

Servant leaders recognize that the best ideas often come from collaboration and the sharing of diverse perspectives. Encourage open communication, teamwork, and the exchange of ideas within your organization. This not only helps to build a sense of community but also leads to more effective problem-solving and decision-making.

Empower Employees:

Give your employees the autonomy and resources they need to succeed in their roles. This may involve providing them with the necessary training, tools, and support, as well as trusting them to make decisions and take ownership of their work. By empowering your employees, you're not only demonstrating your faith in their abilities but also creating an environment where they can grow and excel.

Provide Ongoing Feedback and Support:

Servant leaders are committed to the growth and development of their employees, which requires ongoing feedback, coaching, and mentoring. Make it a priority to provide your team members with regular, constructive feedback, and work together to develop plans for their personal and professional growth.

Practice Self-Reflection and Humility:

As a servant leader, it's essential to continually assess your own actions, decisions, and behaviors to ensure you're putting the needs of your employees first. Be open to feedback from your team members and be willing to adapt your leadership style and approach as needed. Embrace humility by acknowledging your own limitations and the value of the contributions of others.

Prioritize Employee Well-being:
Create a work environment that supports the physical, mental, and emotional well-being of your employees. This may involve offering flexible work arrangements, promoting work-life balance, and providing resources and support for mental health and wellness.

Recognize and Celebrate Success:
Servant leaders take the time to acknowledge and celebrate the achievements of their employees. By recognizing individual and team successes, you're not only boosting morale and motivation but also reinforcing the values and behaviors that contribute to a positive, high-performing work environment.

Lead by Example:
As a servant leader, your actions and behaviors set the tone for your organization. Strive to embody the principles of servant leadership in everything you do, demonstrating empathy, humility, and a genuine commitment to the well-being and

success of your employees.

As you see - servant leadership is a powerful and transformative approach to leading and managing in a totally new way. By putting employees first and prioritizing their well-being, growth, and development, servant leaders create an environment where individuals feel valued, supported, and inspired to contribute their best work.

Consider incorporating servant leadership into your repertoire. At least as a part of it. By doing so, you'll not only foster a more engaged, motivated, and high-performing workforce but also set a powerful example for others to follow.

CHAPTER 6: MINDFUL LEADERSHIP

The importance of mindfulness in leadership Strategies for incorporating mindfulness

Companies, corporations, and their leaders are under immense pressure to deliver results, adapt to new challenges, and navigate complex interpersonal dynamics. Amidst this whirlwind of demands and expectations, it can be all too easy to lose sight of the present moment and become overwhelmed by stress and anxiety.

Mindful leadership is an approach that emphasizes the importance of cultivating mindfulness, self-awareness, and emotional intelligence in order to lead more effectively, make better decisions, and create a positive work environment.

In this chapter, we'll explore the concept of mindful leadership, discuss the importance of mindfulness in leadership, and offer practical strategies for incorporating mindfulness into your leadership practice.

The Importance of Mindfulness in Leadership

Mindfulness, at its core, is the practice of being fully present in the moment, with an open and nonjudgmental awareness of one's thoughts, emotions, and sensations. In recent years, mindfulness has gained increasing recognition as a valuable tool for managing stress, improving well-being, and enhancing performance across various domains, including leadership.

Mindful leaders are those who are able to maintain a clear, focused awareness of the present moment, even in the face of challenges, setbacks, and high-pressure situations. By cultivating mindfulness, leaders can develop a greater understanding of their own thoughts, emotions, and behaviors, as well as those of their employees. This heightened self-awareness and emotional intelligence can lead to numerous benefits for both leaders and their organizations, including:

Improved Decision-Making:
Mindful leaders are better equipped to make thoughtful, informed decisions, as they are less likely to be swayed by emotional reactions or cognitive biases. By maintaining a clear, present-moment awareness, leaders can more accurately

assess the situation at hand, weigh the potential consequences of various actions, and choose the best course of action.

Enhanced Emotional Intelligence:

Mindfulness helps leaders develop greater emotional intelligence, which is the ability to recognize, understand, and manage one's own emotions and those of others. Emotional intelligence is a critical leadership skill, as it enables leaders to build strong relationships, navigate complex interpersonal dynamics, and respond effectively to the emotional needs of their employees.

Increased Resilience:

By cultivating mindfulness, leaders can develop greater resilience in the face of adversity and setbacks. Mindful leaders are better able to manage stress, maintain a positive outlook, and bounce back from challenges, which is essential for long-term success in today's rapidly changing business landscape.

More Effective Communication:

Mindful leaders are better listeners, as they are able to be fully present and attentive during conversations. This leads to more effective communication, as leaders are better able to understand the needs, concerns, and perspectives of their employees, and respond with empathy and understanding.

Greater Employee Engagement:
Mindful leaders create a work environment that fosters trust, open communication, and emotional well-being, which can lead to higher levels of employee engagement, motivation, and satisfaction.

Strategies for Incorporating Mindfulness

So, how can you begin to cultivate mindfulness and incorporate it into your leadership practice? Here are some practical strategies to get you started:

Develop a Regular Mindfulness Practice:
One of the most effective ways to develop mindfulness is through regular practice, such as meditation or other mindfulness exercises. By dedicating time each day to cultivating present-moment awareness, you'll gradually strengthen your ability to maintain mindfulness in your daily life and leadership activities. You can download one of the numerous apps for your smartphone.

Practice Mindful Listening:
Make a conscious effort to be fully present and attentive during conversations with your employees, colleagues, and stakeholders. This means resisting the urge to interrupt, formulating responses, or allowing your mind to wander.

Instead, focus on truly hearing and understanding what the other person is saying, and respond with empathy and consideration. Unfortunately, there are no apps able to help you with this one.

Cultivate Self-Awareness:
Regularly reflect on your thoughts, emotions, and behaviors as a leader, and strive to develop a deeper understanding of how they impact your decision-making, communication, and relationships. This self-awareness can help you identify areas where you may need to adjust your approach or develop new skills.

Incorporate Mindful Pauses:
Throughout your day, make an effort to take brief "mindful pauses" – moments when you intentionally bring your attention back to the present moment, without judgment or evaluation. These pauses can help you stay grounded and focused, even in the face of challenges and distractions.

Foster a Mindful Work Environment:
Encourage mindfulness among your employees by modeling mindful behaviors, creating opportunities for mindfulness training and practice, and promoting a culture of open communication and emotional well-being. By fostering a mindful work environment, you can help your team members develop greater self-awareness, resilience, and emotional intelligence.

Practice Mindful Decision-Making:
When faced with important decisions, take the time to pause, reflect, and bring your full, present-moment awareness to the situation at hand. Consider the potential consequences of various options, and strive to make decisions based on a thoughtful, balanced assessment of the available information, rather than being swayed by emotional reactions or cognitive biases.

Engage in Mindful Self-Care:
As a leader, it's essential to take care of your own well-being, both physically and mentally. Develop a self-care routine that incorporates mindfulness practices, such as meditation, yoga, or deep breathing exercises, to help manage stress, maintain emotional balance, and cultivate a greater sense of well-being.

Mindful leadership is an invaluable approach to leading and managing. By cultivating mindfulness and incorporating it into your leadership practice, you can develop greater self-awareness, emotional intelligence, and resilience, which will ultimately enable you to make better decisions, communicate more effectively, and create a positive, supportive work environment for your employees.

By incorporating mindful leadership into your repertoire – you will not only improve your personal well-being and effectiveness as a leader, but it will also have a profound impact on the well-being, engagement, and success of your organization as a whole.

CHAPTER 7: COLLABORATIVE DECISION MAKING

Sharing power and responsibility
Fostering a culture of collaboration

The ability to make effective decisions is more important than ever. Traditional top-down decision-making models, where leaders hold ultimate authority and make decisions with little input from employees, are increasingly being recognized as outdated and ineffective. Collaborative decision-making, on the other hand, is an approach that emphasizes the sharing of power and responsibility between leaders and employees, fostering a culture of collaboration and harnessing the collective wisdom, creativity, and expertise of the entire organization. In this chapter, we'll explore the concept of collaborative decision-making, discuss the benefits of sharing power and responsibility, and offer practical strategies for fostering a culture of collaboration within your organization.

Sharing Power and Responsibility

Collaborative decision-making is grounded in the belief that the best decisions are often those that emerge from the collective input and insights of a diverse group of individuals. By involving employees in the decision-making process, leaders can gain access to a broader range of perspectives, ideas, and expertise, which can lead to more innovative, effective, and well-informed decisions.

Sharing power and responsibility in the decision-making process not only leads to better decisions but also has numerous benefits for both leaders and employees, including:

Increased Employee Engagement:
When employees are given the opportunity to participate in decision-making, they feel a greater sense of ownership, responsibility, and investment in the organization's success. This increased engagement can lead to higher levels of job satisfaction, motivation, and performance. And it will certainly start a positive spiral of development.

Greater Trust and Mutual Respect:
Collaborative decision-making fosters an

environment of trust and mutual respect between leaders and employees. By demonstrating that their input is valued and taken seriously, leaders can cultivate strong, positive relationships with their team members.

Enhanced Learning and Skill Development:
Participating in the decision-making process provides employees with opportunities to develop critical thinking, problem-solving, and communication skills, contributing to their personal and professional growth.

More Effective Implementation:
Decisions that are made collaboratively are more likely to be effectively implemented, as employees are more committed to and invested in the outcomes. Additionally, because employees have been involved in the decision-making process, they are better equipped to anticipate potential challenges and develop strategies for addressing them.

Fostering a Culture of Collaboration

Creating a culture of collaboration within your organization requires intentional effort, commitment, and ongoing reinforcement. Here are some practical strategies for fostering a collaborative environment and promoting collaborative decision making:

Lead by Example:

As a leader, your actions and behaviors set the tone for your organization. Strive to model collaborative behaviors, such as seeking input from others, being open to feedback, and sharing power and responsibility.

Encourage Open Communication:
Create a work environment where employees feel comfortable voicing their opinions, concerns, and ideas, and where open communication is encouraged and valued. This may involve establishing regular forums for discussion and feedback, such as team meetings, brainstorming sessions, or one-on-one check-ins.

Provide Training and Support:
Offer training and resources to help employees develop the skills and knowledge needed to participate effectively in collaborative decision making. This may include workshops on effective communication, problem-solving, and conflict resolution, as well as access to tools and technologies that facilitate collaboration.

Recognize and Reward Collaborative Behaviors:
Reinforce the importance of collaboration by recognizing and rewarding employees who demonstrate collaborative behaviors and contribute to the organization's decision-making processes. This may involve offering praise, promotions, bonuses, or other forms of recognition for employees who consistently

demonstrate a commitment to collaboration.

Develop Clear Processes and Structures:
Establish clear processes and structures for collaborative decision-making within your organization. This may involve setting up cross-functional teams, creating decision-making frameworks, or implementing collaborative decision-making tools and technologies.

Embrace Diversity and Inclusion:
A diverse workforce brings a wealth of perspectives, ideas, and experiences to the table, which can greatly enrich the decision-making process. Make a conscious effort to promote diversity and inclusion within your organization, and encourage employees from different backgrounds, roles, and areas of expertise to participate in decision-making.

Be Patient and Flexible:
Collaborative decision-making can be time-consuming, and it may require a willingness to compromise, adapt, and consider alternative perspectives. Be patient and flexible as you navigate the collaborative process, and recognize that the benefits of collaborative decision-making often outweigh the challenges.

Evaluate and Reflect on Outcomes:
After decisions have been made collaboratively, take the time to evaluate the outcomes and reflect on the process. This can help you identify areas for

improvement, as well as celebrate successes and reinforce the value of collaboration within your organization.

Collaborative decision-making is a powerful approach to leading and managing in today's complex, interconnected world. Depending only on the manager's or management's point of view can be quite limited and potentially dangerous for the organization.

By sharing power and responsibility with your employees and fostering a culture of collaboration, you can harness the collective wisdom, creativity, and expertise of your entire organization, leading to more effective, well-informed decisions and a stronger, more engaged workforce.

We certainly recommend you that you – at least to some degree – implement this as a part of your unorthodox leadership style. By doing so, you'll not only promote a more inclusive, empowering work environment but also set a powerful example for others to follow.

CHAPTER 8: THE POWER OF VULNERABILITY

Embracing vulnerability as a leader
Building trust and authenticity

If we didn't lose all the traditional managers in the chapter about Servant Leadership – we will probably lose the rest here. But for the open-minded rest of you, we have lots of more good stuff coming up.

For many years, conventional wisdom has dictated that leaders must maintain an image of strength, confidence, and invincibility in order to be respected and effective. However, in recent years, there has been a growing recognition of the power of vulnerability in leadership, as well as the importance of authenticity, empathy, and emotional intelligence in building trust and fostering strong relationships with employees. In this chapter, we'll explore the concept of vulnerability in leadership, discuss the benefits of embracing vulnerability as a leader, and offer practical strategies for building trust and authenticity within your organization.

Embracing Vulnerability as a Leader

Vulnerability can be defined as the willingness to expose oneself to emotional risk, uncertainty, or potential criticism, in the pursuit of growth, connection, and authenticity. As a leader, embracing vulnerability involves acknowledging your own limitations, fears, and imperfections, and being open and honest with your employees about these aspects of your experience.

Embracing vulnerability as a leader can be really challenging and anxiety-provoking, as it requires stepping way outside of your comfort zone, confronting your insecurities, and potentially opening yourself up to criticism or judgment. However, the benefits of embracing vulnerability in leadership are significant and far-reaching, including:

Building Trust:
When leaders are willing to be vulnerable and authentic with their employees, they demonstrate that they trust their team members with their emotions, fears, and imperfections. This, in turn, fosters a climate of trust within the organization, as employees feel more comfortable being open,

honest, and vulnerable themselves.

Enhancing Emotional Intelligence:

Vulnerability is closely linked to emotional intelligence, which is the ability to recognize, understand, and manage one's own emotions and those of others. By embracing vulnerability, leaders can develop greater self-awareness, empathy, and emotional regulation, which are all essential components of effective leadership.

Fostering Authenticity:

Authentic leaders are those who are true to themselves, their values, and their emotions, rather than striving to maintain a facade of perfection or invincibility. Embracing vulnerability allows leaders to be more authentic in their interactions with employees, which can lead to stronger relationships and a greater sense of connection and belonging within the organization.

Encouraging Growth and Innovation:

Vulnerability is an essential ingredient for growth and innovation, as it involves taking risks, embracing uncertainty, and being open to failure. By modeling vulnerability, leaders can create an environment where employees feel empowered to take risks, think creatively, and learn from their mistakes.

Increasing Employee Engagement:

When leaders are vulnerable and authentic,

employees are more likely to feel valued, respected, and understood, which can lead to higher levels of engagement, motivation, and job satisfaction.

Building Trust and Authenticity

So, how can you begin to embrace vulnerability as a leader and foster a culture of trust and authenticity within your organization? Here are some practical strategies to get you started:

Be Open and Honest:
As a leader, strive to be open and honest with your employees about your thoughts, feelings, and experiences, even when doing so feels uncomfortable or risky. This may involve sharing your fears or uncertainties, admitting when you don't have all the answers, or acknowledging your mistakes and taking responsibility for them.

Encourage Emotional Expression:
Create a work environment where employees feel comfortable expressing their emotions, both positive and negative, and where emotional expression is seen as a natural and valuable part of the human experience. This may involve offering training and resources on emotional intelligence, as well as actively encouraging employees to share their feelings and experiences with one another.

Practice Active Listening:
Make a conscious effort to be fully present

and attentive during conversations with your employees, and strive to truly hear and understand their perspectives, emotions, and needs. This not only demonstrates empathy and respect but also fosters trust and connection within your team.

Show Empathy and Compassion:
When your employees share their feelings, challenges, or struggles, respond with empathy, compassion, and understanding, rather than judgment or criticism. This can help create a supportive, nurturing work environment where employees feel valued, respected, and cared for.

Be Willing to Be Wrong:
Acknowledge that you, as a leader, don't always have all the answers and that sometimes you may be wrong. Be open to receiving feedback and constructive criticism from your employees, and be willing to adjust your approach or perspective based on their input.

Model Resilience and Growth Mindset:
Embracing vulnerability also involves being open to failure and learning from your mistakes. Model a resilient, growth-oriented mindset by openly discussing your own failures, setbacks, and lessons learned, and encourage your employees to do the same.

Develop a Support Network:
Vulnerability can be challenging, especially for

leaders who have been conditioned to maintain an image of strength and invincibility. Cultivate a support network of trusted colleagues, mentors, or friends with whom you can share your experiences, emotions, and challenges, and who can offer guidance, encouragement, and perspective as you navigate your leadership journey.

Foster a Culture of Psychological Safety:
Create a work environment where employees feel safe to express themselves openly and honestly, without fear of judgment, ridicule, or retribution. This may involve setting clear expectations and guidelines for respectful communication, addressing instances of incivility or harassment, and promoting a culture of inclusivity, diversity, and respect.

Embracing vulnerability as a leader is a brave, powerful, and transformative approach to leadership that can yield significant benefits for both leaders and employees alike. By being open, honest, and authentic with your team, you can foster a climate of trust, connection, and belonging within your organization, while also promoting growth, innovation, and resilience.

CHAPTER 9: HOLACRACY: A NEW ORGANIZATIONA L STRUCTURE

The principles of holacracy
Case studies and implementation tips

Another innovative and alternative way to navigate the complex business landscape is holacracy. A self-management system that empowers employees, eliminates traditional hierarchies and fosters collaboration and transparency.

In this chapter, we'll explore the principles of holacracy, delve into case studies of organizations that have successfully implemented holacratic systems, and offer practical tips for implementing holacracy within your own organization.

The Principles of Holacracy

Holacracy is a management system that seeks to decentralize power and decision-making authority, distributing it across an organization's employees in a more equal and collaborative manner. Developed by Brian Robertson in the early 2000s, holacracy is based on several key principles, which include:

Self-Organization:

At the core of holacracy is the idea that employees are capable of organizing themselves and making decisions independently, without the need for centralized control or supervision. This empowers individuals and teams to take ownership of their work and to adapt quickly and efficiently to changing circumstances.

Circles and Roles:

In a holacratic organization, work is organized into circles, which are autonomous, self-governing units responsible for specific areas of the business. Each circle is composed of individuals who fill specific roles, which are clearly defined and regularly updated to ensure that the work of the circle remains relevant and aligned with the organization's broader objectives.

Distributed Authority:

Decision-making authority in a holacratic organization is distributed among the circles and roles, rather than being concentrated in a centralized hierarchy. This allows for greater agility, flexibility, and responsiveness, as decisions can be made more quickly and efficiently by those closest to the relevant information and context.

Transparent Governance:
Holacracy emphasizes transparency and open communication in all aspects of the organization's governance, from decision-making processes to resource allocation. This ensures that all members of the organization have access to the information they need to make informed decisions and contribute effectively to the organization's success.

Evolutionary Adaptability:
Holacracy is designed to facilitate continuous learning, growth, and adaptation within the organization. By regularly reviewing and updating roles, processes, and objectives, holacratic organizations can stay nimble and responsive in the face of change and uncertainty.

Case Studies and Implementation Tips

Many organizations have successfully implemented holacracy, yielding a wide range of benefits, including increased agility, adaptability, innovation, and employee engagement. Here are a few notable examples:

Zappos:
The online retailer Zappos, known for its strong emphasis on company culture and customer service, adopted holacracy in 2013. The transition was not without challenges, but the company has reported numerous positive outcomes, including increased cross-functional collaboration, enhanced innovation, and more efficient decision-making processes.

Medium:
The online publishing platform Medium implemented holacracy in 2012, with the aim of fostering greater autonomy, creativity, and adaptability among its employees. The company has since reported increased employee satisfaction, improved collaboration, and a stronger focus on the company's mission and values.

David Allen Company:
The productivity consulting firm David Allen Company adopted holacracy in 2011, in an effort to better align the organization with the principles of its flagship product, the Getting Things Done (GTD) methodology. The company has reported increased efficiency, effectiveness, and employee satisfaction as a result of the transition to holacracy.

If you're considering implementing holacracy

within your own organization, here are some practical tips to guide you through the process:

Start with a Pilot Program:
Before implementing holacracy organization-wide, consider starting with a pilot program in a specific department or team. This can help you gain a better understanding of the challenges and benefits associated with holacracy, and allow you to make adjustments and refinements before rolling it out more broadly.

Invest in Training and Support:
Transitioning to a holacratic system can be a significant shift for many employees, especially those who are accustomed to traditional hierarchical structures. Providing comprehensive training and ongoing support can help ease the transition and ensure that all employees understand the principles, practices, and expectations of the new system.

Establish Clear Roles and Responsibilities:
In a holacratic organization, clearly defined roles and responsibilities are crucial to ensuring that work is distributed effectively and that all employees have a clear understanding of their scope and authority. Take the time to carefully define and document the roles within your organization, and be prepared to update and refine these definitions as needed.

Foster Open Communication and Transparency:

Encourage open, honest communication among all employees and across all levels of the organization. This can help build trust, promote collaboration, and ensure that all employees have access to the information they need to make informed decisions and contribute effectively to the organization's success.

Be Prepared for Resistance and Challenges:
Implementing holacracy can be a challenging process, and not all employees may initially embrace the new system. Be prepared to address resistance and concerns, and to provide support and guidance to help employees adapt to the new way of working.

Regularly Review and Adapt: Holacracy is designed to be an evolving, adaptive system that can respond to changing circumstances and needs. Regularly review your organization's roles, processes, and objectives to ensure that they remain relevant and aligned with the organization's broader goals, and be prepared to make adjustments and refinements as needed.

Lead by Example:
As a leader, it's important to model the principles and practices of holacracy in your own work and interactions with employees. This can help create a culture of trust, collaboration, and empowerment, and demonstrate your commitment to the new system.

Holacracy offers a promising alternative to traditional hierarchical organizational structures, with the potential to increase agility, adaptability, innovation, and employee engagement.

By understanding the principles of holacracy, learning from the experiences of organizations that have successfully implemented the system, and following practical tips for implementation, you can harness the power of holacracy to transform your organization and unlock new levels of success and well-being for your employees.

CHAPTER 10: RADICAL TRANSPARENCY

The benefits of open communication
How to create a transparent workplace

With the heightened expectations from consumers, society, and also its own employees, organizations are increasingly recognizing the importance of fostering a culture of open communication, honesty, and trust.

Radical transparency is an unorthodox leadership and management approach that emphasizes complete openness and honesty in all aspects of an organization's operations, from decision-making processes to resource allocation, performance evaluations, and beyond.

In this chapter, we'll explore the benefits of radical transparency, discuss the challenges associated with implementing this approach, and offer practical tips for creating a transparent workplace that empowers employees, fosters collaboration, and drives organizational success.

The Benefits of Open Communication

Radical transparency offers numerous benefits for organizations and their employees, including:

Enhanced Trust:
By being open and honest with employees about company decisions, goals, and challenges, leaders can build trust and foster a sense of loyalty and commitment among their workforce. Employees are more likely to trust leaders who are transparent and forthcoming, and this trust can lead to increased motivation, engagement, and productivity.

Improved Collaboration:
Transparency fosters a culture of collaboration by breaking down the barriers that often exist between different levels of an organization or between departments. When employees have access to the same information and are encouraged to share their ideas and perspectives openly, they are better able to work together and find innovative solutions to challenges.

Greater Agility:
Transparent organizations are better equipped to adapt to change, as they can make informed decisions more quickly and efficiently. When employees have access to all relevant information,

they can better understand the reasons behind decisions and the implications of those decisions for their own work, allowing them to adapt more easily to new directions or priorities.

Increased Innovation:
A transparent workplace encourages employees to share their ideas, insights, and feedback, fostering a culture of continuous learning and innovation. Employees are more likely to take risks and pursue new ideas when they feel supported and informed by their leaders and colleagues.

Enhanced Employee Satisfaction:
Radical transparency can lead to higher levels of employee satisfaction, as employees feel more valued, respected, and involved in the organization's success. When employees have a clear understanding of the organization's goals and their role in achieving those goals, they are more likely to feel a sense of purpose and fulfillment in their work.

How to Create a Transparent Workplace

Creating a transparent workplace requires a significant shift in mindset and behavior for many leaders and employees, especially those who are accustomed to more traditional, hierarchical organizational structures. Here are some practical tips for fostering radical transparency within your organization:

Set Clear Expectations:
Establish clear expectations for openness and honesty at all levels of the organization. Encourage employees to share their ideas, insights, and concerns openly and without fear of retribution, and be prepared to do the same as a leader.

Be Open and Honest About Decisions:
Communicate openly and honestly about the reasons behind decisions, including the rationale, the data or information that informed the decision, and the expected outcomes. This can help employees understand the context for decisions and how those decisions may impact their work.

Share Information Freely:
Make information and data readily available to all employees, so they can make informed decisions and contribute effectively to the organization's success. This may involve creating a centralized information hub, using collaboration tools and platforms, or holding regular all-hands meetings to share updates and insights.

Encourage Open Dialogue:
Foster a culture of open dialogue by encouraging employees to ask questions, share their perspectives, and offer constructive feedback. Create opportunities for employees to engage in open conversations, such as town hall meetings,

team huddles, or anonymous feedback channels.

Address Challenges Head-On:
Be transparent about the challenges and obstacles your organization is facing, and engage employees in the process of finding solutions. This can help build resilience and foster a sense of ownership and commitment among your workforce.

Practice Humility and Accountability:
As a leader, model humility and accountability by openly acknowledging your own mistakes, limitations, and areas for growth. This can help create a culture where employees feel comfortable admitting their own mistakes and learning from them, ultimately driving continuous improvement and growth.

Involve Employees in Decision-Making:
Encourage greater transparency and collaboration by involving employees in decision-making processes, such as goal-setting, strategy development, and problem-solving. This can help employees feel more invested in the organization's success and more empowered to contribute their ideas and expertise.

Be Transparent About Performance and Compensation:
Foster a culture of openness and fairness by being transparent about performance expectations, evaluations, and compensation. Clearly communicate the criteria used for performance

evaluations, and ensure that employees have access to the information and resources they need to succeed.

Encourage Cross-Functional Collaboration:
Break down silos and encourage collaboration across departments and levels by sharing information, resources, and expertise. This can help create a more cohesive and agile organization that is better equipped to respond to change and capitalize on new opportunities.

Continuously Review and Adjust:
Just as with any leadership approach, it's important to regularly review and adjust your transparency practices to ensure that they continue to support the organization's goals and priorities. Be open to feedback from employees and be prepared to make changes as needed to create a more transparent and inclusive workplace.

The rather radical theory - Radical transparency is an innovative leadership and management approach that offers numerous benefits for organizations, including enhanced trust, improved collaboration, greater agility, increased innovation, and higher levels of employee satisfaction.

By understanding the principles of radical transparency, recognizing the challenges associated with implementation, and following the practical tips outlined in this chapter, you can create a very transparent workplace that empowers employees, fosters collaboration and drives organizational success.

We are aware that this management won't fit everywhere for multiple reasons. But consider how radical transparency might fit into your organization's unique culture and objectives. By embracing openness, honesty, and collaboration, you can unlock the full potential of your employees and set your organization on a path to greater success and well-being in today's rapidly changing business landscape.

CHAPTER 11: ENCOURAGING INNOVATION AND CREATIVITY

Fostering a culture of innovation
Techniques for inspiring creativity

For most organizations, innovation is a question of life and death. If you can foster a culture of innovation and creativity you are better positioned to thrive in the face of change and disruption. Innovative and creative solutions not only help organizations differentiate themselves from competitors but also drive long-term growth and success. In this chapter, we will explore the importance of fostering a culture of innovation, discuss the challenges associated with nurturing creativity, and offer practical tips and techniques for inspiring employees to think and act in new, innovative ways.

The Importance of Fostering a Culture of Innovation

A culture of innovation is one in which employees are encouraged and empowered to explore new ideas, challenge the status quo, and take risks in the pursuit of novel solutions and improvements. Organizations that can successfully foster such a culture are more likely to:

Adapt to Change:
Organizations that embrace innovation are better equipped to adapt to changes in the market, industry, or consumer preferences, ensuring long-term viability and success.

Differentiate Themselves:
Innovative products, services, and processes can help organizations stand out from competitors and capture a greater share of the market.

Attract Top Talent:
A culture of innovation and creativity can be a powerful draw for top talent, who are often drawn to organizations that offer opportunities for growth, learning, and creative expression.

Drive Long-Term Growth:
By continuously exploring new ideas and opportunities, organizations can unlock new sources of revenue, reduce costs, and improve operational efficiency, all of which contribute to

long-term growth and success.

Challenges in Nurturing Creativity

Despite the many benefits of fostering a culture of innovation, organizations often face several challenges in nurturing creativity among their employees:

Fear of Failure:
In many organizations, the fear of failure can be a significant barrier to innovation, as employees may be hesitant to take risks or pursue unproven ideas if they believe that failure will be met with punishment or criticism.

Lack of Time and Resources:
Employees may struggle to find the time and resources needed to explore and develop new ideas, particularly if they are already stretched thin by their existing responsibilities.

Organizational Silos:
In organizations with rigid departmental structures or hierarchies, it can be difficult for employees to collaborate across teams or share ideas and insights, limiting the potential for innovation.

Resistance to Change:
Some employees may be resistant to change or new ways of thinking, particularly if they are comfortable with the status quo or have a vested

interest in maintaining existing processes and structures.

Techniques for Inspiring Creativity

Despite these challenges, organizations can take several practical steps to foster a culture of innovation and inspire employees to think creatively:

Encourage Experimentation:
Foster a culture that encourages experimentation and risk-taking, and make it clear that failure is an acceptable and even necessary part of the innovation process. This can help employees feel more comfortable taking risks and pursuing new ideas.

Provide Time and Resources:
Give employees the time and resources they need to explore and develop new ideas. This may involve creating dedicated innovation teams, setting aside time for brainstorming or idea generation sessions, or providing funding and resources for employee-driven innovation projects.

Break Down Silos:
Encourage cross-functional collaboration by breaking down organizational silos and creating opportunities for employees from different departments or teams to work together on projects or initiatives. This can help to promote the sharing of ideas and insights and foster a more

innovative and creative organizational culture.

Offer Training and Support:
Provide training and support to help employees develop the skills and mindset needed for creative thinking and innovation. This may involve offering workshops on creative problem-solving, design thinking, or other innovation methodologies, or providing access to mentoring, coaching, or other forms of support.

Recognize and Reward Innovation:
Recognize and reward employees for their innovative ideas and contributions, regardless of whether those ideas ultimately lead to success. This can help to create a positive feedback loop that encourages employees to continue exploring new ideas and taking risks. Offer both financial and non-financial rewards and incentives, such as public recognition, promotions, or opportunities for professional development.

Create a Supportive Environment:
Cultivate a work environment that supports and encourages creativity and innovation. This may involve providing physical spaces designed for brainstorming and collaboration, offering flexible work schedules, or implementing policies that support work-life balance and employee well-being.

Encourage Diverse Perspectives:
Foster diversity and inclusion within your

organization, as diverse perspectives can lead to more innovative and creative solutions. Create opportunities for employees with different backgrounds, experiences, and perspectives to collaborate and contribute their unique insights.

Model Innovation from the Top:
As a leader, demonstrate your commitment to innovation by actively exploring new ideas, taking risks, and learning from failures. By modeling innovative behavior, you can inspire employees to do the same.

Promote a Growth Mindset:
Encourage a growth mindset among employees by emphasizing the importance of continuous learning and personal development. Offer opportunities for employees to learn and grow, such as training programs, workshops, or access to industry events and conferences.

Solicit Employee Input:
Actively seek input and ideas from employees at all levels of the organization, and create channels for employees to share their suggestions, feedback, and insights. This can help to generate a steady stream of new ideas and foster a sense of ownership and engagement among employees.

Fostering a culture of innovation and creativity is essential for organizations looking to thrive in a rapidly changing business environment. By understanding the importance of innovation, recognizing the challenges associated with nurturing creativity, and implementing the practical techniques outlined in this chapter, leaders can inspire employees to think and act in new, innovative ways that drive long-term growth and success.

By cultivating a culture that embraces new ideas, challenges the status quo, and supports risk-taking, you can unlock the full potential of your employees and set your organization on a path to greater success.

CHAPTER 12: STRENGTHS-BASED LEADERSHIP

Identifying and leveraging employee strengths Building high-performance teams

Now we arrived at a topic that will be sweet music for most A-type managers = Strength-Based Management. In a competitive business environment, organizations must continually strive to improve their performance and achieve better results. One innovative approach to achieving this goal is through strengths-based leadership, which focuses on identifying and leveraging the unique strengths and talents of individual employees. By building on the natural strengths of team members, organizations can create high-performance teams that are better equipped to overcome challenges and achieve outstanding results. In this chapter, we will explore the principles of strengths-based leadership, discuss the benefits of this approach, and offer practical tips for identifying employee strengths and building high-performance teams.

The Principles of Strengths-Based Leadership

Strengths-based leadership is grounded in the belief that every individual possesses a unique set of strengths, talents, and abilities that can be harnessed to achieve outstanding results. By focusing on these strengths rather than on weaknesses or areas for improvement, leaders can empower employees to achieve their full potential and contribute to the organization's success in meaningful ways. The key principles of strengths-based leadership include:

Every individual has unique strengths:
Recognize that each employee brings a distinct set of strengths and talents to the organization. These strengths may be related to their skills, knowledge, experiences, or personal attributes, and can contribute to the organization's success in various ways.

Strengths can be developed and honed:
While individuals may have innate strengths, they can also develop and refine these strengths through practice, learning, and experience.

Provide employees with opportunities to build on their strengths and apply them in new and challenging contexts.

Focus on strengths rather than weaknesses:
Shift the focus from fixing weaknesses or addressing gaps in performance to building on existing strengths and maximizing their potential. This can help to create a more positive and empowering work environment, as well as boost employee morale, engagement, and productivity.

Strengths-based teams are more effective:
High-performance teams are those that can effectively leverage the unique strengths of each team member to achieve common goals. By aligning individual strengths with team objectives, leaders can create more cohesive, agile, and effective teams.

The Benefits of Strengths-Based Leadership

Strengths-based leadership offers several important benefits for organizations and employees, including:

Improved Employee Engagement:
By focusing on their strengths, employees are more likely to feel engaged and motivated in their work, as they can see how their unique talents

contribute to the organization's success.

Higher Productivity:
Employees who are encouraged to leverage their strengths are more likely to be productive, as they are working in areas where they naturally excel and can achieve better results with less effort.

Increased Job Satisfaction:
Employees who are able to use their strengths in their work are more likely to feel satisfied and fulfilled in their roles, as they can experience a greater sense of accomplishment and meaning in their work.

Enhanced Team Performance:
High-performance teams that effectively leverage the strengths of each team member are better equipped to overcome challenges, adapt to change, and achieve outstanding results.

Greater Retention:
Employees who feel valued for their strengths and are given opportunities to develop and apply these strengths are more likely to remain with the organization, reducing turnover and associated costs.

Identifying and Leveraging Employee Strengths

To harness the benefits of strengths-based leadership, leaders must first be able to identify and understand the unique strengths of each employee. This process can involve a combination of observation, feedback, and formal assessments, such as:

Observe Employees in Action:
Watch employees as they work and look for patterns of behavior or areas of expertise that may indicate strengths or talents. Take note of tasks or activities that employees seem to excel at or enjoy, as well as any positive feedback or recognition they receive from peers or supervisors.

Solicit Feedback from Colleagues and Supervisors: Ask colleagues and supervisors for their insights and observations about the strengths and talents of individual employees. This can help to provide a more comprehensive and accurate understanding of each employee's unique strengths.

Conduct Strengths Assessments: Utilize formal assessments or tools, such as the CliftonStrengths assessment, to help employees identify and understand their unique strengths and talents. These assessments can provide valuable insights and serve as a starting point for strengths-based development and coaching.

Engage in Open Dialogue: Have open and honest conversations with employees about their strengths, asking them about their passions, interests, and areas where they feel they excel.

This can help to create a deeper understanding of each employee's strengths and how they can be leveraged within the organization.

Once employee strengths have been identified, leaders can take several steps to leverage these strengths and build high-performance teams:

Align Strengths with Roles and Responsibilities:
Assign tasks and responsibilities to employees based on their strengths, ensuring that each individual is working in areas where they can excel and contribute most effectively to the team's success.

Foster a Strengths-Based Culture:
Encourage a culture that values and celebrates individual strengths, providing ongoing recognition and support for employees who excel in their areas of strength. This can help to create a more positive and empowering work environment that fosters engagement, productivity, and growth.

Encourage Strengths-Based Development:
Provide opportunities for employees to develop and refine their strengths, offering training, mentoring, and coaching to help individuals hone their talents and apply them in new and challenging contexts.

Facilitate Cross-Functional Collaboration:
Encourage collaboration between employees with

complementary strengths, creating opportunities for individuals to learn from one another and work together to achieve common goals.

Continuously Reevaluate and Adapt:
Regularly review and reassess the strengths of individual team members, as well as the alignment between strengths and roles or responsibilities. Be prepared to make adjustments as needed to ensure that each employee is working in areas where they can contribute most effectively to the team's success.

Strengths-based leadership offers a powerful and effective approach to building high-performance teams and driving organizational success. By focusing on the unique strengths and talents of each employee, leaders can create a more engaged, productive, and satisfied workforce that is better equipped to overcome challenges and achieve outstanding results.

CHAPTER 13: ADAPTIVE LEADERSHIP

Navigating change and uncertainty
Developing adaptability in your team

The ability to navigate change and uncertainty is not only good for a captain of a ship or a pilot of an airplane. It has also become a critical leadership skill. Adaptive leadership is an approach that equips leaders to effectively manage change, overcome challenges, and capitalize on opportunities by fostering a culture of adaptability and resilience within their teams.

In this chapter, we will explore the principles of adaptive leadership, discuss the importance of adaptability in today's business landscape, and provide practical tips for developing adaptive leadership skills and cultivating adaptability within your team.

The Principles of Adaptive Leadership

Adaptive leadership is a leadership style that emphasizes flexibility, responsiveness, and the ability to make informed decisions in the face of change and uncertainty. The key principles of adaptive leadership include:

Embrace Change:
Recognize that change is an inherent part of today's business environment, and adopt a mindset that views change as an opportunity for growth and development rather than as a threat or challenge. Change and crises create possibilities for those who can adapt.

Foster a Learning Culture:
Encourage a culture of continuous learning and development, providing employees with opportunities to acquire new skills, expand their knowledge, and adapt to changing circumstances.

Encourage Experimentation and Innovation:
Support and encourage employees to explore new ideas, take risks, and learn from failures. This can help to foster a culture of adaptability and resilience and ensure that your organization remains agile and responsive to change.

Develop Emotional Intelligence:
Enhance your emotional intelligence and

empathy, as these skills are critical for effective adaptive leadership. This includes the ability to recognize and manage your own emotions, as well as understanding and responding effectively to the emotions of others.

Communicate Effectively:
Clearly communicate your organization's vision, goals, and expectations, and ensure that your team has the information and resources they need to adapt to changing circumstances and make informed decisions.

The Importance of Adaptability in Today's Business Landscape

The ability to adapt to change and uncertainty is essential for organizations seeking to thrive in a rapidly changing business environment. Organizations that are able to quickly and effectively respond to new challenges, capitalize on emerging opportunities, and navigate uncertainty are better positioned to achieve long-term success and maintain a competitive edge.

Adaptability is important for several reasons, including:

Accelerating Pace of Change:
The pace of change in today's business environment is faster than ever before, driven by technological advancements, shifting consumer

preferences, and increasing global competition. Organizations must be able to adapt quickly to remain relevant and competitive.

Increasing Complexity:

The business environment has become increasingly complex, with organizations facing a myriad of challenges and opportunities. Adaptive leaders are able to effectively navigate this complexity and make informed decisions in the face of uncertainty.

Growing Workforce Diversity:

Today's workforce is more diverse than ever before, with employees representing a wide range of backgrounds, experiences, and perspectives. Adaptive leaders are able to effectively manage this diversity and leverage the unique strengths and talents of their team members.

Developing Adaptability in Your Team

To cultivate adaptability within your team and develop your adaptive leadership skills, consider the following strategies:

Model Adaptability:

As a leader, demonstrate your own adaptability by embracing change, learning from setbacks, and remaining open to new ideas and perspectives. By modeling adaptive behavior, you can inspire your team to do the same.

Encourage Continuous Learning:

Foster a learning culture within your organization, providing employees with opportunities to acquire new skills, expand their knowledge, and develop their adaptive capabilities. This may involve offering training programs, workshops, or access to industry events and conferences.

Support and Encourage Experimentation:

Create an environment that supports and encourages experimentation and innovation, allowing employees to take risks, explore new ideas, and learn from their mistakes. This can help to foster a culture of adaptability and resilience and ensure that your organization remains agile and responsive to change.

Promote Open Communication:

Establish open lines of communication within your team, encouraging employees to share their ideas, concerns, and feedback. This can help to identify potential challenges and opportunities and enable your team to adapt more effectively to changing circumstances.

Provide Clear Direction and Support:

Clearly articulate your organization's vision, goals, and expectations, and provide the necessary resources and support to help your team navigate change and uncertainty. This may involve setting realistic expectations, offering guidance and coaching, and ensuring that employees have access to the information and resources they need to adapt and succeed.

Encourage Collaboration and Teamwork:
Foster a collaborative work environment, encouraging employees to work together, share ideas, and learn from one another. This can help to create a more adaptable and resilient team that is better equipped to overcome challenges and capitalize on emerging opportunities.

Develop Emotional Intelligence:
Enhance your emotional intelligence and empathy, as these skills are critical for effective adaptive leadership. This includes the ability to recognize and manage your own emotions, as well as understanding and responding effectively to the emotions of others.

Recognize and Reward Adaptability:
Acknowledge and celebrate employees who demonstrate adaptability and resilience in the face of change and uncertainty. This can help to reinforce the importance of adaptability and encourage others to develop these skills.

Regularly Assess and Adjust:
Periodically evaluate your team's adaptability and responsiveness to change, identifying areas for improvement and making any necessary adjustments to your leadership approach or

organizational processes. This can help to ensure that your team remains agile and adaptable in the face of ongoing change and uncertainty.

Adaptive leadership is an essential skill for today's leaders, as it equips them to effectively navigate change and uncertainty and capitalize on emerging opportunities. By embracing the principles of adaptive leadership and fostering a culture of adaptability within your team, you can help to ensure that your organization remains agile, resilient, and well-positioned for long-term success.

CHAPTER 14: THE POWER OF STORYTELLING

Harnessing stories to inspire and motivate
Crafting compelling narratives

Now you might think – where did that come from? It is story time now. Yes – exactly.

Storytelling has been an integral part of human culture and communication for thousands of years. From ancient myths and legends to modern-day movies and novels, stories have the power to captivate, inspire, and motivate like no other form of communication.

As a leader, harnessing the power of storytelling can be an invaluable tool for engaging your team, articulating your vision, and driving change within your organization. In this chapter, we will explore the importance of storytelling in leadership, discuss strategies for crafting compelling narratives, and provide practical tips for using storytelling to inspire and motivate your team.

The Importance of Storytelling in Leadership

Storytelling is an essential leadership skill for several reasons:

Emotional Connection:
Stories have the unique ability to evoke emotions and create a sense of connection and empathy. By telling stories, leaders can build emotional connections with their team members, which can lead to increased engagement, motivation, and loyalty.

Simplifying Complex Ideas:
Storytelling can help leaders simplify complex ideas and concepts, making them more accessible and relatable to their audience. By framing information within the context of a story, leaders can enhance understanding and facilitate learning.

Sharing Values and Vision:
Stories are an effective way for leaders to communicate their values, vision, and goals, creating a shared sense of purpose and direction within their team. Through storytelling, leaders can help their team members understand the "why" behind their work and inspire them to work

towards a common goal.

Persuasion and Influence:
Storytelling is a powerful tool for persuasion and influence, as it allows leaders to present information in a way that is both engaging and memorable. By crafting compelling narratives, leaders can more effectively influence the opinions, behaviors, and decisions of their team members.

Inspiring Action:
Stories have the power to inspire action and drive change within organizations. By sharing stories of success, failure, and learning, leaders can motivate their team members to take risks, embrace change, and strive for continuous improvement.

Crafting Compelling Narratives

To harness the power of storytelling in your leadership, it's essential to develop the ability to craft compelling narratives. Consider the following strategies as you work to refine your storytelling skills:

Know Your Audience:
Before crafting a story, take the time to understand your audience, considering their interests, needs, and values. This will allow you to create a narrative that resonates with your team members and speaks to their unique experiences and perspectives.

Establish a Clear Purpose:
Determine the purpose of your story, whether it be to inspire, motivate, educate, or entertain. By establishing a clear objective, you can ensure that your narrative remains focused and relevant to your audience.

Create a Strong Structure:
Effective stories typically follow a three-act structure, consisting of a beginning, middle, and end. In the beginning, introduce your characters and set the stage for your story. In the middle, build tension and conflict as your characters face challenges and obstacles. Finally, in the end, resolve the conflict and provide a satisfying conclusion.

Be Authentic: Authenticity is crucial for effective storytelling. Share personal experiences, emotions, and insights, and avoid exaggerating or fabricating details. By being genuine and vulnerable, you can build trust and credibility with your audience.

Use Descriptive Language: To create a vivid and engaging narrative, use descriptive language and sensory details to paint a picture in your audience's mind. This can help your listeners to better visualize and connect with your story.

Using Storytelling to

Inspire and Motivate

Once you have developed your storytelling skills, consider the following strategies for using storytelling to inspire and motivate your team:

Share Personal Stories: Share personal stories that demonstrate your values and beliefs, providing your team with insight into your character and leadership style. By sharing your own experiences, you can inspire your team to embrace your vision, take risks, and learn from their mistakes.

Highlight Success Stories:
Share stories of success and achievement, both within your organization and from external sources. By highlighting examples of individuals or teams overcoming challenges and achieving their goals, you can inspire your team to strive for greatness and believe in their own potential.

Emphasize Learning and Growth:
Use storytelling to illustrate the importance of learning, growth, and continuous improvement. Share stories of failure and setbacks, emphasizing the lessons learned and the growth that resulted from overcoming adversity. This can encourage your team to view challenges as opportunities for growth and development.

Encourage Team Members to Share Their Stories:
Invite your team members to share their own stories, creating a culture of open communication

and mutual support. This can help to build trust, foster collaboration, and enhance the sense of community within your team.

Use Metaphors and Analogies:
Metaphors and analogies can help to simplify complex ideas and make them more relatable to your audience. By drawing comparisons between your message and familiar concepts or experiences, you can create a more engaging and memorable narrative.

Incorporate Storytelling into Meetings and Presentations:
Integrate storytelling into your regular meetings and presentations, using stories to illustrate key points and concepts. This can help to create a more engaging and memorable experience for your team members and enhance their understanding of the information being presented.

Leverage Storytelling in Change Management:
Storytelling can be a powerful tool in driving organizational change. By sharing stories that illustrate the need for change, the benefits of the proposed changes, and the potential risks of maintaining the status quo, you can help your team members to understand and embrace the change process.

The power of storytelling is an invaluable tool for leaders seeking to inspire and motivate their teams. By developing your storytelling skills and incorporating storytelling into your leadership approach, you can create emotional connections with your team members, simplify complex ideas, and drive change within your organization.

Consider how the power of storytelling fits into your unorthodox leadership cocktail and how it can enhance your ability to engage, inspire, and motivate your team.

CHAPTER 15: GAMIFICATION IN MANAGEMENT

Engaging employees through gamification
Implementing game-based strategies

Gamification is the process of applying game design elements and principles to non-game contexts, such as business management and employee engagement. By integrating aspects of games, such as competition, rewards, and progress tracking, leaders can create more engaging and motivating work environments for their teams.

In this chapter, we will explore the benefits of gamification in management, discuss strategies for implementing game-based approaches, and provide practical tips for engaging employees through gamification.

The Benefits of Gamification in Management

Gamification offers several potential benefits for leaders and organizations, including:

Increased Engagement:
Gamification can create a more engaging work environment, helping to capture employees' attention and encourage active participation in tasks and projects.

Enhanced Motivation:
By incorporating elements of competition, rewards, and progress tracking, gamification can foster intrinsic motivation, encouraging employees to take ownership of their work and strive for continuous improvement.

Improved Learning and Skill Development:
Gamification can facilitate learning and skill development by making the process more enjoyable and interactive. By presenting information in a game-based format, leaders can enhance understanding and retention, helping employees to develop the skills and knowledge they need to succeed in their roles.

Collaboration and Team Building:
Many gamification strategies involve teamwork and collaboration, which can help to build relationships, enhance communication, and foster

a sense of camaraderie within teams.

Greater Performance and Productivity:
By engaging and motivating employees, gamification can lead to increased performance and productivity. As employees become more invested in their work and strive to achieve goals and objectives, they are likely to be more efficient and effective in their roles.

Implementing Game-Based Strategies

To harness the benefits of gamification in your management approach, consider the following strategies for implementing game-based techniques within your organization:

Set Clear Goals and Objectives:
Establish clear goals and objectives for your gamification efforts, ensuring that they align with your organization's broader mission and values. This will help to ensure that your gamification initiatives are focused, purposeful, and relevant to your team's needs.

Incorporate Various Game Elements:
Integrate a variety of game elements into your gamification strategy, such as points, badges, leaderboards, and progress tracking. By incorporating multiple elements, you can create a more engaging and immersive experience for your employees.

Create a Sense of Competition:
Foster a healthy sense of competition within your team by implementing leaderboards, achievement badges, and performance-based rewards. This can help to motivate employees to perform at their best and strive for continuous improvement.

Provide Regular Feedback and Recognition:
Offer frequent feedback and recognition to your employees, celebrating their achievements and progress. This can help to reinforce the importance of the game-based strategies and encourage employees to continue participating in the activities.

Customize the Experience:
Tailor your gamification initiatives to the unique needs and preferences of your team, taking into account factors such as job roles, skill levels, and individual interests. This will help to ensure that your game-based strategies are relevant and engaging for all employees.

Engaging Employees through Gamification

To effectively engage your employees through gamification, consider the following tips and best practices:

Align Gamification with Organizational Goals:
Ensure that your gamification initiatives align

with your organization's overall goals and objectives. This will help to create a sense of purpose and direction for your employees, motivating them to participate in the game-based activities.

Focus on Intrinsic Motivation:

While extrinsic rewards, such as points and badges, can be effective in motivating employees, it's essential to also focus on fostering intrinsic motivation. Encourage employees to take ownership of their work, set personal goals, and strive for self-improvement.

Provide Opportunities for Collaboration and Teamwork:

Design your gamification initiatives to encourage collaboration and teamwork among your employees. This can help to foster a sense of camaraderie and unity within your team, while also promoting the development of communication and problem-solving skills.

Ensure Fairness and Transparency:

In order for your gamification strategies to be effective, they must be perceived as fair and transparent by your employees. Establish clear rules and guidelines for the game-based activities, and ensure that all employees have equal access to resources and opportunities for success.

Continuously Monitor and Adjust:

Regularly evaluate the effectiveness of your

gamification initiatives, gathering feedback from your employees and monitoring key performance metrics. Use this information to make adjustments and improvements to your game-based strategies, ensuring that they continue to engage and motivate your team.

Make it Fun and Enjoyable:

While gamification can be a powerful tool for driving employee engagement and motivation, it's essential to maintain a sense of fun and enjoyment. Create game-based activities that are enjoyable and entertaining for your employees, and avoid placing too much emphasis on competition and performance metrics.

Support Employee Development:

Use your gamification initiatives as an opportunity to support the professional development of your employees. Provide resources, training, and opportunities for skill-building in conjunction with your game-based activities, helping your employees to grow and advance in their careers.

Encourage Employee Input:

Involve your employees in the design and implementation of your gamification strategies, seeking their input and ideas. This can help to ensure that your game-based initiatives are relevant and engaging for your team, while also fostering a sense of ownership and involvement.

Who would have thought this just a few years back – but gamification offers a unique and innovative approach to management, providing leaders with an opportunity to engage and motivate their employees through game-based strategies. By incorporating elements of competition, rewards, and progress tracking, leaders can create more engaging and motivating work environments, leading to increased performance and productivity.

CHAPTER 16: EMOTIONAL INTELLIGENCE IN LEADERSHIP

Understanding and managing emotions
Building emotionally intelligent teams

Emotional intelligence (EI) is another critical aspect of effective leadership, encompassing the ability to recognize, understand, manage, and use emotions effectively in both ourselves and others. Emotionally intelligent leaders are more capable of navigating complex social situations, building strong relationships, and fostering positive work environments.

In this chapter, we will explore the importance of emotional intelligence in leadership, discuss strategies for understanding and managing emotions, and provide guidance on building emotionally intelligent teams.

The Importance of Emotional Intelligence in Leadership

Emotional intelligence is an essential leadership skill, offering several key benefits for leaders and their organizations, including:

Improved Communication:
Emotionally intelligent leaders are better equipped to understand and interpret the emotions and needs of their team members, enabling them to communicate more effectively and build stronger relationships.

Enhanced Decision-Making:
By recognizing and managing their own emotions, as well as those of others, emotionally intelligent leaders can make more informed and balanced decisions, taking into account both rational and emotional factors.

Increased Empathy and Compassion:
Leaders with high emotional intelligence are more empathetic and compassionate, allowing them to better support their team members and foster a positive work environment.

Greater Adaptability and Resilience:
Emotionally intelligent leaders are better able to adapt to changing circumstances and cope with stress, helping them to remain resilient in the face of challenges and setbacks.

Improved Conflict Resolution:
Emotionally intelligent leaders are more skilled at resolving conflicts and addressing interpersonal issues, promoting harmony and collaboration within their teams.

Understanding and Managing Emotions

To develop your emotional intelligence as a leader, it is essential to learn how to recognize, understand, and manage emotions, both in yourself and others. Consider the following strategies for enhancing your emotional intelligence:

Practice Self-Awareness:
Cultivate self-awareness by regularly reflecting on your emotions, thoughts, and behaviors. This can help you to better understand your emotional patterns, triggers, and reactions, enabling you to manage your emotions more effectively.

Develop Empathy:
Practice empathy by actively listening to your team members, striving to understand their emotions, perspectives, and needs. This can help you to build stronger relationships, enhance communication, and better support your team members.

Learn to Manage Your Emotions:

Develop techniques for managing your emotions, such as deep breathing, meditation, or journaling. By learning to regulate your emotions, you can improve your decision-making, communication, and overall effectiveness as a leader.

Practice Active Listening:
Enhance your active listening skills by giving your full attention to your team members, paraphrasing their words, and asking clarifying questions. This can help you to better understand their emotions and needs, and respond more effectively to their concerns.

Understand the Role of Emotions in Decision-Making:
Recognize the impact of emotions on decision-making, and strive to consider both rational and emotional factors when making decisions. This can help you to make more balanced and informed choices, leading to better outcomes for your organization.

Building Emotionally Intelligent Teams

In addition to developing your own emotional intelligence, it is essential to foster emotional intelligence within your team. Consider the following strategies for building emotionally intelligent teams:

Model Emotional Intelligence:
Demonstrate emotional intelligence in your own leadership, modeling empathy, self-awareness, and effective emotion management for your team members. This can help to create a positive work environment and encourage your team members to develop their own emotional intelligence.

Provide Training and Development:
Offer training and development opportunities for your team members, focusing on emotional intelligence skills such as communication, empathy, and emotion management. This can help to enhance the overall emotional intelligence of your team and improve their effectiveness in their roles.

Foster a Supportive Work Environment:
Create a supportive work environment that encourages open communication, collaboration, and emotional expression. This can help to promote emotional intelligence within your team and foster stronger relationships among team members.

Encourage Emotional Expression:
Encourage your team members to express their emotions openly and honestly, both in one-on-one conversations and in group settings. By creating a safe space for emotional expression, you can help to promote emotional intelligence and enhance communication within your team.

Provide Regular Feedback and Coaching:
Offer regular feedback and coaching to your team members, focusing on both their emotional intelligence skills and their overall performance. This can help to reinforce the importance of emotional intelligence and support the ongoing development of these skills within your team.

Develop a Culture of Empathy:
Foster a culture of empathy within your organization, encouraging team members to support and care for one another. This can help to create a more emotionally intelligent workforce and promote a positive work environment.

Address Conflict Proactively:
Address conflict proactively and constructively, using emotionally intelligent strategies to resolve disagreements and maintain harmony within your team. By modeling effective conflict resolution, you can help to enhance the emotional intelligence of your team and promote a more collaborative work environment.

Recognize and Reward Emotional Intelligence:
Recognize and reward team members who demonstrate strong emotional intelligence skills, such as empathy, active listening, and effective emotion management. This can help to reinforce the importance of emotional intelligence and encourage the ongoing development of these skills within your team.

Emotional intelligence offers numerous benefits for leaders and their organizations. By developing your own emotional intelligence and fostering emotional intelligence within your team, you can enhance communication, improve decision-making, and create a more positive and supportive work environment.

CHAPTER 17: PURPOSE-DRIVEN LEADERSHIP

Aligning Values with organizational goals
Inspiring purpose in your team

Purpose-driven leadership is an approach to management that focuses on aligning individual and organizational values with the overarching goals and mission of the organization. By inspiring a sense of purpose in their team members, purpose-driven leaders can create a more motivated, engaged, and committed workforce, leading to improved performance and productivity. In this chapter, we will explore the importance of purpose-driven leadership, discuss strategies for aligning values with organizational goals, and provide guidance on inspiring purpose in your team.

The Importance of Purpose-Driven Leadership

Purpose-driven leadership offers several key benefits for leaders and their organizations, including:

Increased Employee Engagement:
When employees feel a strong sense of purpose and alignment with their organization's values and goals, they are more likely to be engaged and committed to their work, leading to improved performance and productivity.

Enhanced Employee Retention:
Employees who feel a sense of purpose in their work are more likely to remain with their organization, reducing turnover and associated costs.

Improved Decision-Making:
Purpose-driven leaders are better able to make strategic decisions that align with their organization's values and goals, ensuring long-term success and sustainability.

Stronger Organizational Culture:
By fostering a sense of purpose and shared values within their teams, purpose-driven leaders can create a more cohesive and supportive organizational culture.

Greater Resilience and Adaptability:
Purpose-driven organizations are more resilient and adaptable, as employees are more committed to overcoming challenges and achieving shared goals.

Aligning Values with Organizational Goals

To practice purpose-driven leadership, it is essential to align your values and those of your team members with the goals and mission of your organization. Consider the following strategies for achieving this alignment:

Clarify Your Organization's Mission and Values:
Clearly articulate your organization's mission and values talking to emotions, ensuring that they are well-defined and easily understood. This can help to create a strong foundation for purpose-driven leadership and guide decision-making at all levels of your organization.

Assess Your Personal Values:
Reflect on your own personal values and consider how they align with those of your organization. By understanding and embracing your values, you can become a more authentic and purpose-driven leader.

Communicate Your Values and Goals:
Regularly communicate your organization's

values and goals to your team members, reinforcing their importance and ensuring that they are understood and embraced by all.

Align Individual Goals with Organizational Goals:

Work with your team members to set individual goals that align with the broader goals of your organization. This can help to create a sense of purpose and commitment among your team members, while also ensuring that their efforts are focused on achieving shared objectives.

Recognize and Reward Value-Driven Behavior:

Recognize and reward team members who demonstrate behavior that aligns with your organization's values and goals. This can help to reinforce the importance of purpose-driven leadership and encourage the ongoing development of these behaviors within your team.

Inspiring Purpose in Your Team

In addition to aligning values and goals, purpose-driven leaders must also inspire a sense of purpose in their team members. Consider the following strategies for inspiring purpose within your team:

Share Compelling Stories:

Share compelling stories that illustrate the impact of your organization's work, helping to connect your team members to the broader mission and goals. This can help to create a sense of purpose and motivate them to contribute to the organization's success.

Connect Individual Efforts to Organizational Success:

Help your team members understand how their individual efforts contribute to the overall success of your organization, creating a clear link between their work and the organization's mission and goals.

Encourage Employee Input and Participation:

Involve your team members in the decision-making process and seek their input on strategic initiatives, fostering a sense of ownership and involvement in the organization's success. This can help to create a sense of purpose and commitment among your team members.

Foster a Culture of Growth and Development:

Encourage your team members to continuously learn and develop their skills, promoting a culture of growth and development within your organization. This can help to create a sense of purpose and fulfillment among your team members, as they feel valued and supported in their personal and professional growth.

Support Work-Life Balance:

Promote a healthy work-life balance within your organization, recognizing that employees are more likely to feel a sense of purpose and commitment to their work when they feel supported in their personal lives. This may include offering flexible work arrangements, promoting wellness initiatives, or providing resources to help employees manage stress and achieve balance.

Provide Opportunities for Meaningful Contributions:

Offer opportunities for your team members to make meaningful contributions to your organization's mission and goals, whether through special projects, cross-functional teams, or volunteer initiatives. This can help to create a sense of purpose and fulfillment, as employees feel that their efforts are making a difference.

Be a Role Model:

As a purpose-driven leader, strive to be a role model for your team members, embodying your organization's values and demonstrating a strong sense of purpose in your own work. This can help to inspire and motivate your team members, encouraging them to adopt a similar mindset.

Encourage Collaboration and Teamwork:

Foster a collaborative and supportive work environment, where team members feel encouraged to work together towards shared goals. This can help to create a sense of purpose and unity among your team members, as they work together to achieve success.

Purpose-driven leadership brings numerous benefits for leaders and their organizations.

By aligning personal values with organizational goals, and inspiring a sense of purpose in your team, you can create a more motivated, engaged, and committed workforce, leading to improved performance and productivity.

CHAPTER 18: REMOTE AND FLEXIBLE WORK LEADERSHIP

Adapting to the new normal
Effective strategies for remote management

The modern workplace has undergone significant changes in recent years, with pandemics, wars, and inflation – and that uncertainty will probably keep on for years to come.

Remote and flexible work becoming increasingly prevalent. The rise of remote work has been accelerated by the global pandemic, forcing many organizations to adapt to new ways of working and prompting leaders to develop new strategies for managing remote teams effectively. In this chapter, we will explore the challenges and opportunities associated with remote and flexible work leadership, as well as discuss effective strategies for remote management.

Adapting to the New Normal

As organizations have shifted to remote work arrangements, leaders have faced numerous challenges and opportunities in adapting to this new normal. Some of the most significant challenges associated with remote work leadership include:

Maintaining Communication:
Effective communication is essential for successful leadership, but remote work can make it more difficult to maintain open lines of communication with team members.

Building and Maintaining Trust:
Trust is a critical component of effective leadership, but remote work can create challenges in building and maintaining trust among team members.

Ensuring Accountability and Productivity:
Remote work can make it more difficult for leaders to monitor employee performance and ensure accountability and productivity.

Fostering Collaboration and Teamwork:
Remote work can create barriers to collaboration and teamwork, as employees may not have the same opportunities to interact and work together as they would in a traditional office setting.

Managing Work-Life Balance:
Remote work can blur the lines between work and personal life, making it difficult for employees to maintain a healthy work-life balance.

Despite these challenges, remote work also presents great opportunities for leaders to develop new skills and strategies for managing their teams effectively. Some of the key opportunities associated with remote work leadership include:

Access to a Broader Talent Pool:
Remote work allows organizations to access a broader talent pool, as they are not limited by geographic constraints.

Increased Flexibility:
Remote work offers increased flexibility for employees, which can lead to higher levels of job satisfaction and retention.

Cost Savings:
Remote work can lead to cost savings for organizations, as they can reduce overhead costs associated with maintaining physical office spaces.

Effective Strategies for Remote Management

To be successful in leading remote and flexible work teams, leaders must develop and implement effective strategies for remote management. Consider the following strategies for managing remote teams effectively:

Establish Clear Expectations:

Clearly communicate your expectations for remote work, including performance standards, communication protocols, and deadlines. This can help to ensure that your team members understand their responsibilities and can work effectively in a remote setting.

Leverage Technology:

Utilize technology to facilitate communication, collaboration, and productivity among your remote team members. This may include using video conferencing tools, project management software, and instant messaging platforms.

Maintain Regular Communication:

Establish regular communication with your remote team members, using a variety of channels to stay connected and ensure that everyone is kept informed of important updates and developments.

Foster a Culture of Trust:

Build trust among your remote team members by being transparent, maintaining open lines of communication, and demonstrating your commitment to their success.

Encourage Collaboration and Teamwork:

Create opportunities for your remote team members to collaborate and work together, leveraging technology to facilitate teamwork and encourage a sense of unity among your team.

Provide Support and Resources:
Ensure that your remote team members have access to the necessary resources and support to be successful in their roles, including adequate technology, training, and professional development opportunities.

Monitor Performance and Provide Feedback:
Regularly monitor the performance of your remote team members and provide constructive feedback to help them grow and improve.

Promote Work-Life Balance:
Encourage your remote team members to maintain a healthy work-life balance, offering support and resources to help them manage stress and maintain personal well-being.

Offer Recognition and Rewards:
Acknowledge and celebrate the accomplishments and contributions of your remote team members, offering recognition and rewards that reflect their hard work and dedication. This can help to maintain morale and motivation among your remote workforce.

Stay Connected and Build Relationships:
Make an effort to stay connected and build

relationships with your remote team members, even if you are not physically present in the same location. This can help to foster a sense of belonging and unity among your team, despite the physical distance.

Be Adaptable and Open to Change:
Remote work arrangements often require a high degree of adaptability and openness to change. Be prepared to adjust your leadership style and strategies as needed to accommodate the unique challenges and opportunities associated with remote work.

Encourage Employee Development:
Provide opportunities for your remote team members to grow and develop professionally, offering access to training programs, mentorship, and other resources that can help them to build the skills and knowledge needed to succeed in their roles.

Create a Sense of Belonging:
Foster a sense of belonging among your remote team members by creating opportunities for social interaction and team-building activities, even if they are conducted virtually. This can help to maintain a strong sense of team unity and cohesion, despite the challenges posed by remote work.

It is clear to all that remote and flexible work leadership presents unique challenges and opportunities for leaders. By adapting to the new normal and implementing effective strategies for remote management, leaders can harness the benefits of remote work while overcoming the associated challenges.

CHAPTER 19: INCLUSIVE LEADERSHIP

The importance of diversity and inclusion
Creating an inclusive work environment

Inclusive leadership has become increasingly important in today's diverse and globalized workforce. Embracing diversity and fostering an inclusive work environment can provide numerous benefits for organizations, including increased creativity and innovation, improved decision-making, higher employee engagement, and better financial performance.

In this chapter, we will explore the importance of diversity and inclusion in leadership and discuss strategies for creating an inclusive work environment.

The Importance of Diversity and Inclusion

Diversity and inclusion have become essential components of effective leadership in the modern workplace. A diverse workforce brings together a wide range of perspectives, experiences, and skills, which can help to drive innovation, creativity, and problem-solving. Moreover, fostering an inclusive work environment can help to attract and retain top talent, improve employee engagement, and create a more positive workplace culture. Some of the key benefits of diversity and inclusion in leadership include:

Enhanced Creativity and Innovation:
A diverse workforce can contribute to greater creativity and innovation, as employees with different backgrounds, experiences, and perspectives can generate a broader range of ideas and solutions.

Improved Decision-Making:
Research has shown that diverse teams make better decisions, as they are more likely to consider multiple perspectives, challenge assumptions, and engage in constructive debate.

Higher Employee Engagement:
Employees who feel valued and included in their workplace are more likely to be engaged, motivated, and committed to their organization's success.

Better Financial Performance:

Studies have found a correlation between companies with diverse leadership teams and higher financial performance, suggesting that inclusive leadership can contribute to an organization's bottom line.

Increased Talent Attraction and Retention:
Organizations that prioritize diversity and inclusion are more likely to attract and retain top talent, as employees increasingly seek out employers that value and support their unique perspectives and experiences.

Creating an Inclusive Work Environment

To capitalize on the benefits of diversity and inclusion, leaders must create an inclusive work environment where all employees feel valued, respected, and supported. Consider the following strategies for fostering an inclusive workplace culture:

Lead by Example:
As a leader, it is essential to model inclusive behavior and set the tone for your organization. Demonstrate your commitment to diversity and inclusion through your actions, communications, and decision-making.

Establish a Clear Vision and Strategy:
Develop a clear vision and strategy for

diversity and inclusion within your organization, outlining specific goals, objectives, and action plans. Communicate this vision to your team and ensure that all employees understand their role in contributing to a more inclusive work environment.

Provide Education and Training:
Offer education and training to help employees understand the importance of diversity and inclusion, as well as the impact of unconscious bias, stereotypes, and discrimination. Encourage ongoing learning and development in this area to promote greater awareness and understanding among your team.

Foster Open Dialogue:
Create opportunities for open dialogue and discussion around diversity and inclusion, encouraging employees to share their experiences, perspectives, and ideas. Listen to and value the input of all team members and work together to identify and address any issues or concerns.

Implement Inclusive Policies and Practices:
Review and update your organization's policies and practices to ensure that they are inclusive and supportive of all employees, regardless of their background, identity, or experience. This may include offering flexible work arrangements, implementing diversity recruitment strategies, or providing resources and support for

underrepresented groups.

Celebrate and Value Differences:
Recognize and celebrate the diverse perspectives, experiences, and contributions of your employees, creating a culture where differences are valued and appreciated.

Encourage Mentorship and Sponsorship:
Promote mentorship and sponsorship opportunities within your organization, helping employees from diverse backgrounds to develop their skills, build their networks, and advance their careers.

Measure and Track Progress:
Establish metrics and benchmarks to measure and track your organization's progress in achieving its diversity and inclusion goals. Regularly assess your progress and make adjustments as needed to ensure that you are moving toward a more inclusive work environment.

Hold Leaders Accountable:
Ensure that leaders at all levels of your organization are held accountable for promoting diversity and inclusion, both in their own teams and across the organization as a whole. Establish clear expectations and provide regular feedback on their performance in this area.

Create Employee Resource Groups (ERGs):
Support the establishment of employee resource

groups, which can provide valuable resources, networking opportunities, and support for employees from diverse backgrounds. ERGs can also play a critical role in promoting diversity and inclusion within your organization by serving as advocates, advisors, and change agents.

Address Microaggressions and Bias:

Be aware of and address any instances of microaggressions or unconscious bias that may occur within your organization. Encourage employees to speak up when they witness or experience these behaviors and take appropriate action to address and prevent them from happening in the future.

Promote Collaboration and Teamwork:

Encourage collaboration and teamwork across your organization, bringing together diverse perspectives and experiences to drive innovation, creativity, and problem-solving. By fostering a culture of inclusivity, you can help to break down barriers and promote greater understanding and appreciation of diversity.

Recognize the Intersectionality of Identities:

Understand that individuals often hold multiple, intersecting identities, and recognize the unique challenges and experiences that this can present. Be mindful of these complexities when developing and implementing diversity and inclusion initiatives.

Be Open to Feedback and Continuous Improvement:

Recognize that creating an inclusive work environment is an ongoing process and be open to feedback and continuous improvement. Regularly solicit input from your employees and be willing to make changes as needed to ensure that your organization remains committed to fostering a diverse and inclusive workplace.

By embracing the principles of inclusive leadership and implementing these strategies, you can create a work environment where all employees feel valued, respected, and supported, regardless of their background, identity, or experience. In doing so, you can harness the many benefits of diversity and inclusion, driving innovation, creativity, and success for your organization in today's increasingly diverse and globalized workforce.

CHAPTER 20: CROSS-CULTURAL LEADERSHIP

Navigating cultural differences
Building bridges and fostering understanding

Navigating cultural differences and fostering understanding among diverse team members is essential for effective leadership and organizational success. In this chapter, we will explore the importance of cross-cultural leadership and discuss strategies for building bridges and fostering understanding among team members from different cultural backgrounds.

The Importance of Cross-Cultural Leadership

As organizations continue to expand their global reach, leaders must be prepared to work with and manage diverse teams with team members from various cultural backgrounds. Cross-cultural leadership involves understanding and appreciating different cultural values, beliefs, and communication styles, and using this knowledge to create a harmonious and effective work environment. The benefits of effective cross-cultural leadership include:

Enhanced Collaboration:
By understanding and respecting cultural differences, leaders can foster greater collaboration and teamwork among diverse team members, enabling them to work together more effectively to achieve common goals.

Improved Communication:
Cross-cultural leadership helps improve communication by breaking down language barriers and misunderstandings that may arise due to differences in communication styles, norms, and expectations.

Greater Adaptability:
Leaders who possess strong cross-cultural skills are better equipped to adapt to new situations and challenges that may arise when working with diverse teams or in international settings.

Increased Innovation:
Diverse teams with members from different cultural backgrounds can generate a broader range of ideas and perspectives, leading to increased

innovation and creativity.

Enhanced Reputation:
Organizations with leaders who demonstrate strong cross-cultural leadership abilities are likely to be viewed more favorably by clients, partners, and stakeholders in the global marketplace.

Building Bridges and Fostering Understanding

To succeed in cross-cultural leadership, leaders must be able to build bridges and foster understanding among team members from different cultural backgrounds. The following strategies can help leaders develop and enhance their cross-cultural leadership skills:

Develop Cultural Intelligence:
Cultural intelligence refers to the ability to understand, appreciate, and adapt to different cultures. To develop cultural intelligence, leaders should educate themselves about different cultures, norms, and values, and strive to understand how these factors may influence their team members' behaviors, expectations, and communication styles.

Practice Active Listening:
Active listening is a critical skill for effective cross-cultural communication. By listening attentively to what others are saying, asking clarifying

questions, and reflecting on what has been said, leaders can gain a deeper understanding of their team members' perspectives and needs.

Be Mindful of Communication Styles:

Different cultures have different communication styles, and being aware of these differences can help leaders avoid misunderstandings and communicate more effectively with their team members. For example, some cultures may value directness and assertiveness, while others may prioritize harmony and indirect communication.

Encourage Open Dialogue:

Fostering an environment where team members feel comfortable discussing their cultural backgrounds, experiences, and perspectives can promote greater understanding and appreciation of diversity. Encourage open dialogue and create opportunities for team members to share their stories and learn from one another.

Show Empathy and Understanding:

Demonstrating empathy and understanding towards team members from different cultural backgrounds can help to build trust and rapport, leading to stronger working relationships and a more cohesive team.

Be Aware of Cultural Stereotypes and Biases:

Recognize and challenge any cultural stereotypes or biases that you may hold, and encourage your team members to do the same. By actively working to overcome these biases, leaders can create a more inclusive and supportive work environment for all team members.

Leverage Diversity for Innovation:
Encourage your diverse team members to share their unique perspectives and ideas, and leverage this diversity to drive innovation and creativity within your organization.

Adapt Your Leadership Style:
Recognize that different cultures may have different expectations regarding leadership styles and behaviors. Be willing to adapt your leadership style to better accommodate the needs and preferences of your diverse team members.

Provide Cultural Training:
Offer cultural training and education programs for your team members to help them better understand and appreciate different cultures, norms, and values. This can also help to reduce misunderstandings and foster greater collaboration among diverse team members.

Celebrate Cultural Diversity:
Recognize and celebrate the cultural diversity within your team, and use this as an opportunity to learn from one another and build stronger working relationships. Organize team-building activities that incorporate elements from different cultures or host cultural events to showcase and celebrate the unique backgrounds of your team

members.

Establish Clear Expectations:
Clearly communicate your expectations regarding teamwork, communication, and performance to ensure that all team members understand what is expected of them, regardless of their cultural background. This can help to prevent misunderstandings and promote greater alignment within the team.

Be Patient and Flexible:
Recognize that working with a diverse team can sometimes present challenges and require additional time and effort to overcome cultural differences and misunderstandings. Be patient and flexible in your approach, and be prepared to invest the necessary time and resources to ensure the success of your cross-cultural team.

By embracing these strategies, leaders can effectively navigate the complexities of cross-cultural leadership and foster greater understanding, collaboration, and success within their diverse teams.

As the world becomes more interconnected and organizations continue to expand globally, the ability to lead across cultures will become increasingly important for leaders at all levels. By developing strong cross-cultural leadership skills, you can position yourself and your organization for success in today's increasingly diverse and globalized workforce.

CHAPTER 21: REVERSE MENTORING

Learning from younger employees
Embracing multigenerational perspectives

Our organizations are becoming more diverse and multigenerational than ever before. As a result, leaders must find innovative ways to tap into the unique skills, perspectives, and insights that each generation brings to the table. One such approach is reverse mentoring, where younger employees mentor their more experienced counterparts.

In this chapter, we will explore the concept of reverse mentoring, discuss its benefits, and offer strategies for embracing multigenerational perspectives in the workplace.

The Concept of Reverse Mentoring

Reverse mentoring is a leadership development practice that flips the traditional mentoring model on its head. In a traditional mentoring relationship, a more experienced employee mentors a younger, less experienced colleague, providing guidance, support, and sharing their knowledge and expertise. In reverse mentoring, the roles are reversed, with younger employees mentoring their more experienced counterparts.

This approach acknowledges that younger employees possess valuable skills, perspectives, and insights that can benefit their more experienced colleagues, particularly in areas such as technology, social media, and emerging market trends. Reverse mentoring can help bridge the generational gap in the workplace, fostering greater understanding and collaboration among employees of all ages and experience levels.

The Benefits of Reverse Mentoring

Reverse mentoring offers several benefits for both younger and more experienced employees, as well as the organization as a whole. Some of these benefits include:

Enhanced Learning and Skill Development:
Reverse mentoring allows more experienced employees to learn about new technologies, trends, and best practices from their younger colleagues, helping them to stay current and relevant in their roles. At the same time, younger employees can develop their leadership,

communication, and coaching skills through the mentoring process.

Greater Collaboration and Teamwork:
By fostering relationships between employees of different generations, reverse mentoring can break down barriers and promote greater collaboration and teamwork within the organization.

Improved Engagement and Retention:
Reverse mentoring can help to improve employee engagement and retention, particularly among younger employees who may feel more valued and connected to the organization as a result of their mentoring relationships.

Increased Innovation and Creativity:
By bringing together diverse perspectives and experiences, reverse mentoring can spark new ideas and drive innovation within the organization.

Enhanced Organizational Culture:
Reverse mentoring can help to create a more inclusive and supportive organizational culture, where employees of all ages and experience levels feel valued, respected, and empowered to contribute their unique skills and perspectives.

Embracing Multigenerational Perspectives

To implement a successful reverse mentoring

program and leverage the benefits of multigenerational perspectives, consider the following strategies:

Develop a Clear Program Structure:
Develop a clear structure and process for your reverse mentoring program, including goals, objectives, and expected outcomes. Clearly communicate the purpose and benefits of the program to all employees, and establish guidelines for the mentoring relationship, such as meeting frequency, duration, and confidentiality.

Select Participants Carefully:
Identify potential mentors and mentees based on their skills, expertise, and potential areas of growth. Ensure that both parties are open to learning from one another and are committed to the mentoring process.

Provide Training and Support:
Offer training and support for both mentors and mentees to help them navigate the mentoring relationship effectively. This may include workshops on communication, coaching, and feedback, as well as resources and tools to help facilitate the mentoring process.

Establish Clear Goals and Objectives:
Encourage mentors and mentees to establish clear goals and objectives for their mentoring relationship, and regularly review their progress toward these goals. This will help ensure that

both parties are focused on achieving meaningful outcomes and that the mentoring relationship remains aligned with the overall objectives of the program.

Foster a Culture of Learning and Growth:
Create an organizational culture that values learning, growth, and continuous improvement, and encourages employees at all levels to share their knowledge and expertise with one another. This can help to create an environment in which reverse mentoring can thrive, as employees will be more open to learning from one another and embracing diverse perspectives.

Monitor and Evaluate the Program:
Regularly monitor and evaluate the effectiveness of your reverse mentoring program, gathering feedback from participants and making any necessary adjustments to improve the program's success. This may involve conducting surveys, interviews, or focus groups to gather insights and identify areas for improvement.

Celebrate Successes:
Recognize and celebrate the successes and achievements of your reverse mentoring program, sharing success stories and acknowledging the contributions of mentors and mentees. This can help to reinforce the value of the program and encourage ongoing participation and engagement.

Encourage Informal Mentoring Relationships:

In addition to formal reverse mentoring programs, encourage employees to seek out informal mentoring relationships with colleagues of different generations. This can help to further foster a culture of learning and growth within the organization, as employees learn from one another and share their unique perspectives and insights.

Address Potential Challenges:
Be prepared to address potential challenges that may arise in the reverse mentoring process, such as resistance from more experienced employees or difficulties in navigating generational differences. Offer support and guidance to help mentors and mentees overcome these challenges and maintain a positive, productive mentoring relationship.

Continuously Evolve the Program:
As your organization and workforce continue to evolve, it's essential to continuously review and update your reverse mentoring program to ensure it remains relevant and effective. This may involve incorporating new technologies, tools, or methodologies to support the mentoring process or adapting the program to meet the changing needs of your workforce.

By using reverse mentoring in your organization, you tap into much more skills and talents. And you motivate much more too. You probably have a multigenerational workforce in your organization and with this strategy, you can tap into the unique skills, perspectives, and insights of all generations – not only the more experienced part.

By implementing a successful reverse mentoring program and embracing the benefits of diverse perspectives, leaders can drive greater collaboration, innovation, and success within their organizations. As the business landscape continues to evolve and the workforce becomes increasingly diverse, the ability to effectively leverage the power of multigenerational perspectives will become increasingly critical for leaders at all levels.

CHAPTER 22: THE ART OF DELEGATION

Mastering effective delegation
Empowering employees and building trust

Effective delegation is an essential leadership skill that allows leaders to maximize their team's potential, promote employee growth, and ensure the timely completion of tasks and projects. You might think that delegation isn't anything new and unorthodox. However, many leaders struggle with delegation, either due to a lack of trust in their employees or a desire to maintain control over every aspect of their work.

In this chapter, we will explore the art of delegation, discussing strategies for mastering effective delegation, empowering employees, and building trust within your team.

The Importance of Delegation

Delegation is the process of assigning tasks, responsibilities, and decision-making authority to others within your team or organization. It involves not only the act of handing off tasks but also the ability to provide clear instructions, expectations, and support to ensure the successful completion of those tasks.

Delegation is crucial for several reasons:

Time Management:
Leaders have limited time and resources, and delegation allows them to focus on their core responsibilities and strategic priorities, while entrusting others to handle tasks that may be more suited to their skills or expertise.

Employee Development:
Delegation provides opportunities for employees to develop new skills, gain experience, and increase their confidence and competence in their roles. This, in turn, can lead to increased job satisfaction, engagement, and retention.

Team Performance:
Effective delegation promotes teamwork, collaboration, and shared ownership of tasks and projects, leading to increased efficiency, productivity, and overall team performance.

Leadership Development:

Delegation is an essential leadership skill, and the ability to delegate effectively can help leaders grow and advance in their careers.

Mastering Effective Delegation

To become a master delegator, consider the following strategies:

Know Your Team:
Understand the strengths, weaknesses, and capabilities of your team members. This will enable you to delegate tasks appropriately, ensuring that each individual is well-suited to the task at hand and has the necessary skills and resources to complete it successfully.

Set Clear Expectations:
When delegating tasks, provide clear instructions and expectations regarding the desired outcomes, deadlines, and any specific requirements or guidelines that should be followed. This will help to ensure that employees understand what is expected of them and can work towards these goals with confidence.

Provide the Necessary Resources:
Ensure that employees have access to the resources, tools, and information they need to complete their assigned tasks. This may include providing training, access to relevant data, or support from other team members.

Establish Accountability:
Assign responsibility for the completion of tasks and hold employees accountable for their work. Establish regular check-ins or progress updates to ensure that tasks are on track and address any issues or concerns that may arise.

Offer Support and Guidance:
Provide ongoing support and guidance to employees as they work on their delegated tasks, offering assistance and encouragement as needed. Be available to answer questions, address concerns, and provide feedback to help employees stay on track and succeed in their assigned tasks.

Trust Your Team:
Trust your employees to complete their assigned tasks and resist the urge to micromanage or take over the task yourself. By demonstrating trust in your team, you can empower them to take ownership of their work and perform at their best.

Empowering Employees and Building Trust

Effective delegation is built on a foundation of trust and empowerment. To create a workplace culture that fosters trust and empowers employees to take on delegated tasks with confidence, consider the following strategies:

Develop a Trusting Relationship:

Build strong, trusting relationships with your employees by demonstrating honesty, transparency, and openness in your communication and actions. Show that you value their opinions and input and are willing to listen and learn from their perspectives.

Recognize and Reward Success:
Acknowledge and celebrate the successes and achievements of your team members, both individually and as a group.
This can help to reinforce the value of their work, boost morale, and encourage ongoing commitment to their tasks and the overall success of the team.

Encourage Autonomy:
Give employees the freedom to determine how they will complete their assigned tasks, allowing them to develop their own strategies and problem-solving techniques. This can help to build their confidence, foster creativity, and promote a sense of ownership over their work.

Provide Opportunities for Growth:
Encourage employees to develop their skills and expertise by offering opportunities for training, professional development, and exposure to new challenges. This can help to demonstrate your investment in their success and create a supportive environment in which employees feel empowered to grow and excel.

Foster Open Communication:
Create a culture of open communication in which employees feel comfortable sharing their ideas, concerns, and feedback. Encourage dialogue, invite input, and be receptive to suggestions and constructive criticism. This can help to build trust and foster a sense of collaboration and shared ownership within the team.

Model Effective Delegation:
Demonstrate your own commitment to effective delegation by consistently delegating tasks and responsibilities to your team members. This can help to set the tone for your team and establish expectations regarding the importance and value of delegation.

Be Patient:
Recognize that employees may need time to adjust to new tasks or responsibilities, and be patient as they navigate the learning curve. Offer support and encouragement as needed, and be prepared to adjust your expectations or provide additional guidance as necessary.

Did you learn something new? The art of delegation is a crucial leadership skill that can help to maximize the potential of your team, promote employee growth, and ensure the timely completion of tasks and projects. By mastering effective delegation, empowering employees, and building trust within your team, you can create a supportive and collaborative work environment that fosters success, innovation, and growth. As a leader, your ability to effectively delegate tasks and responsibilities will not only enhance your own performance but also contribute to the overall success and well-being of your team and organization.

CHAPTER 23: CELEBRATING FAILURE

Reframing failure as a learning opportunity
Encouraging experimentation and risk-taking

Things are going fast – and at times TOO fast. Innovation often involves taking risks, pushing boundaries, and embracing the possibility of failure. Rather than viewing failure as something to be avoided at all costs, it is crucial for leaders to reframe failure as a learning opportunity and encourage experimentation and risk-taking within their teams.

In this chapter, we will explore the importance of celebrating failure, discuss strategies for reframing failure as a learning opportunity, and offer suggestions for fostering a culture of experimentation and risk-taking.

The Importance of

Celebrating Failure

A fear of failure can stifle creativity, limit innovation, and prevent individuals and organizations from reaching their full potential. By celebrating failure and recognizing its inherent value, leaders can help to create a supportive environment in which employees feel empowered to take risks, learn from their mistakes, and grow both personally and professionally. This can lead to increased innovation, resilience, and overall success within the organization.

Some key benefits of celebrating failure include:

Fostering Innovation:
Embracing failure encourages a culture of experimentation, where employees are more willing to test new ideas, challenge conventional thinking, and push the boundaries of what is possible. This can lead to the development of groundbreaking products, services, and strategies that drive organizational success.

Promoting Learning and Growth:
When failure is viewed as a learning opportunity, employees are more likely to reflect on their experiences, identify areas for improvement, and apply these insights to future endeavors. This can help to drive continuous learning and growth, both on an individual and organizational level.

Enhancing Resilience:

Encountering and overcoming failure can help to build resilience, enabling employees to bounce back more quickly from setbacks and develop the mental and emotional fortitude needed to navigate the challenges of today's business world.

Building Trust and Collaboration:
Celebrating failure can help to create an open and supportive environment in which employees feel comfortable sharing their ideas, concerns, and feedback. This can foster greater trust, collaboration, and shared ownership within the team, ultimately leading to better performance and results.

Reframing Failure as a Learning Opportunity

To create a culture that embraces failure and recognizes its value, leaders must first reframe their own mindset around failure and model this new perspective for their teams. Consider the following strategies for reframing failure as a learning opportunity:

Shift Your Mindset:
Begin by acknowledging and accepting that failure is an inevitable part of the innovation process. Recognize that failure can provide valuable insights and opportunities for growth and development, and strive to view each setback as a learning experience.

Encourage Reflection and Learning:
When failures occur, encourage employees to reflect on their experiences, identify the lessons learned, and consider how these insights can be applied to future efforts. This can help to reinforce the value of failure as a learning opportunity and promote continuous improvement.

Share Your Own Failures:
As a leader, be open and transparent about your own failures, sharing your experiences and the lessons you've learned along the way. This can help to create a culture of openness and vulnerability, where employees feel more comfortable discussing their own setbacks and challenges.

Recognize and Reward Effort:
Rather than focusing solely on results, recognize and reward employees for their effort, dedication, and willingness to take risks. This can help to create a supportive environment in which employees feel valued and appreciated, even when their efforts do not lead to immediate success.

Encouraging Experimentation and Risk-Taking

In addition to reframing failure as a learning opportunity, it is essential for leaders to foster a culture of experimentation and risk-taking within their teams. Consider the following strategies for encouraging employees to take risks and embrace the possibility of failure:

Create a Safe Environment:
Establish a supportive and non-judgmental atmosphere where employees feel comfortable taking risks, sharing their ideas, and discussing their challenges and setbacks. Encourage open communication and promote a culture of trust and mutual respect.

Set Clear Expectations:
Make it clear to your team that taking risks and embracing failure are integral aspects of the innovation process. Encourage employees to be bold in their thinking and to pursue ambitious goals, while also being prepared for the possibility of setbacks and challenges along the way.

Encourage Collaboration and Cross-Pollination:
Foster a collaborative environment where employees can work together, share ideas, and learn from one another. Encourage cross-functional collaboration and the sharing of knowledge and expertise, as this can help to spark innovation and fuel creative problem-solving.

Provide Resources and Support:
Ensure that employees have the resources, tools, and support they need to take risks and experiment with new ideas. This may include offering training and development opportunities,

providing access to cutting-edge technology, or allocating time and resources for employees to pursue innovative projects and initiatives.

Celebrate and Learn from Failures:
When failures do occur, take the time to recognize and celebrate the effort and learning that took place. Share the lessons learned with the team and discuss how these insights can be applied to future endeavors. This can help to reinforce the value of failure as a learning opportunity and encourage ongoing experimentation and risk-taking.

Monitor and Adjust:
Keep track of the progress and results of your team's risk-taking and experimentation efforts, and be prepared to make adjustments as needed. This may involve reevaluating goals, reallocating resources, or providing additional guidance and support to help employees overcome challenges and achieve success.

Celebrating failure and embracing the inherent value of setbacks and challenges can play a critical role in fostering innovation, promoting learning and growth, and driving organizational success. By reframing failure as a learning opportunity and encouraging experimentation and risk-taking within your team, you can create a supportive and dynamic work environment that nurtures creativity, resilience, and high performance. As a leader, your ability to recognize and embrace the potential of failure can not only help to propel your organization forward but also inspire and empower your employees to reach their full potential.

CHAPTER 24: DEVELOPING INTUITION IN LEADERSHIP

Cultivating your inner wisdom
Using intuition to make better decisions"

In today's increasingly complex and unpredictable business landscape, leaders are often faced with making critical decisions under conditions of uncertainty and ambiguity. While data and rational analysis are essential components of the decision-making process, there is growing recognition that intuition—our innate ability to draw on our inner wisdom and experience—can also play a vital role in guiding effective leadership.

In this chapter, we will explore the importance of developing intuition in leadership, discuss strategies for cultivating your inner wisdom, and offer suggestions for using intuition to make better decisions.

The Importance of Intuition in Leadership

Intuition is often described as a gut feeling, an instinct, or a sense of knowing that arises without conscious reasoning. While some may view intuition as mysterious or unscientific, research has shown that intuition is grounded in our brain's ability to rapidly process vast amounts of information and draw on past experiences to make informed decisions.

In the context of leadership, intuition can provide valuable insights and guidance, particularly in situations where information is limited, or the optimal course of action is unclear. Some key benefits of developing intuition in leadership include:

Enhancing Decision-Making:
Intuition can help leaders to quickly assess complex situations, identify potential risks and opportunities, and make informed decisions that align with their values and goals.

Boosting Creativity and Innovation:
By tapping into their inner wisdom, leaders can gain fresh perspectives and insights that inspire creative problem-solving and innovative thinking.

Building Trust and Authenticity:

When leaders are in tune with their intuition, they are better able to connect with their authentic selves and build trust with their teams and stakeholders.

Navigating Uncertainty and Change:
In times of uncertainty and rapid change, intuition can serve as a valuable compass, helping leaders to adapt their strategies, navigate challenges, and seize new opportunities.

Cultivating Your Inner Wisdom

Developing intuition in leadership begins with cultivating your inner wisdom and learning to trust your instincts. Consider the following strategies for honing your intuitive abilities:

Practice Mindfulness and Self-Awareness:
Becoming more attuned to your intuition requires developing a heightened sense of self-awareness. Regularly practicing mindfulness techniques, such as meditation, deep breathing, or journaling, can help you to become more in tune with your thoughts, feelings, and instincts.

Reflect on Your Experiences:
Make a habit of regularly reflecting on your experiences, both successes and failures, to identify patterns, insights, and lessons learned. Over time, this practice can help you to sharpen your intuition and develop a deeper understanding of your leadership style and

decision-making processes.

Develop Your Emotional Intelligence:
Emotional intelligence, or the ability to understand and manage emotions, is closely linked to intuition. By developing your emotional intelligence, you can become more attuned to the subtle cues and signals that inform your intuitive decision-making.

Listen to Your Body:
Our bodies can provide valuable feedback and insights when it comes to intuition. Pay attention to physical sensations, such as a tightness in your chest or a fluttering in your stomach, as these may be signals that your intuition is trying to guide you.

Embrace Uncertainty:
Developing intuition involves embracing uncertainty and learning to trust your instincts, even when the path forward is unclear. Practice stepping outside of your comfort zone and taking calculated risks, and be open to the possibility that your intuition may lead you in unexpected directions.

Using Intuition to Make Better Decisions

Once you have cultivated your inner wisdom, you can begin to apply your intuition to the decision-making process. Consider the following suggestions for using intuition to make better decisions:

Balance Intuition with Analysis:
While intuition can provide valuable insights and guidance, it is important to strike a balance between intuitive and analytical decision-making. Use data and rational analysis to inform your decisions, but also remain open to the insights and perspectives that your intuition can offer.

Trust Your Gut, But Verify:
When faced with a decision, listen to your gut instincts, but also take the time to gather additional information, consult with trusted advisors, and consider alternative perspectives. This approach can help to validate your intuition and ensure that your decisions are well-informed and grounded in reality.

Create Space for Intuition:
In our fast-paced, information-driven world, it can be challenging to find the time and space to tap into our intuition. Be intentional about carving out quiet moments for reflection, meditation, or simply sitting with your thoughts. This can help to create the mental and emotional space needed for your intuition to emerge.

Develop Your Intuitive Vocabulary:
As you become more in tune with your intuition, you may begin to notice that it communicates

with you in different ways. Some people experience intuition as a physical sensation, while others receive visual images, auditory cues, or emotional impressions. Learn to recognize and interpret your intuitive vocabulary, and develop a language for describing and communicating your insights to others.

Be Patient and Persistent:
Developing intuition in leadership is an ongoing process that requires patience, persistence, and a willingness to learn from your experiences. Over time, you will likely find that your intuitive abilities become more refined and reliable, and that you are better equipped to navigate the complex challenges and opportunities that come your way.

Intuition can serve as a powerful tool for enhancing leadership effectiveness, particularly in today's rapidly changing and uncertain business environment. By cultivating your inner wisdom, learning to trust your instincts, and finding ways to integrate intuition into your decision-making processes, you can become a more adaptive, authentic, and impactful leader.

CHAPTER 25: CONCLUSION - BECOMING AN UNSHAKABLE LEADER

Embracing your unique leadership style
Committing to growth and self-improvement

Throughout this book, we have explored a wide range of unorthodox and innovative leadership approaches that can help you become a more effective, inspiring, and adaptable leader in the modern world.

From hands-off leadership and the inverted management pyramid to mindfulness, storytelling, and emotional intelligence, these concepts all have one thing in common: they challenge conventional wisdom and encourage leaders to think outside the box.

Some of them you might know, and others may have provoked you. But we hope it all inspired you to take some of it and use it in your work as a manager.

In this concluding chapter, we will discuss the importance of embracing your unique leadership style and committing to growth and self-improvement on your journey toward becoming an unshakable leader.

Embracing Your Unique Leadership Style

One of the key takeaways from our exploration of unorthodox leadership approaches is that there is no one-size-fits-all solution to effective leadership. Each of the approaches discussed in this book offers valuable insights and strategies that can be adapted to suit your unique strengths, values, and goals as a leader.

By embracing your unique leadership style and incorporating the techniques that resonate most with you, you can create a powerful and authentic leadership presence that inspires trust, loyalty, and high performance in your team.

To begin embracing your unique leadership style, consider the following steps:

Reflect on Your Core Values:

Your core values serve as the foundation for your leadership style, guiding your actions, decisions, and interactions with others. Take some time to identify and articulate your core values and consider how they align with the various leadership approaches discussed in this book.

Identify Your Strengths and Areas for Growth:

As you review the different leadership approaches, consider which ones come naturally to you and which ones may require further development. By recognizing your strengths and areas for growth, you can create a more balanced and well-rounded leadership style.

Experiment with Different Techniques:

Don't be afraid to experiment with different leadership techniques and strategies. Keep an open mind and be willing to try new approaches, even if they feel uncomfortable at first. With practice, you may discover that certain techniques become more effective and aligned with your unique style.

Seek Feedback from Your Team:

Your team can be a valuable source of feedback and insight as you work to develop your unique leadership style. Encourage open and honest communication and be receptive to constructive criticism. Use this feedback to refine and enhance your leadership approach.

Adapt and Evolve:

Embracing your unique leadership style is

an ongoing process that requires continuous learning, adaptation, and growth. Be open to new ideas and experiences, and continually seek opportunities to expand your knowledge and skillset.

Committing to Growth and Self-Improvement

Becoming an unshakable leader is not a destination, but rather a lifelong journey of growth and self-improvement. By committing to ongoing personal and professional development, you can continue to evolve as a leader, adapt to changing circumstances, and inspire your team to reach new heights.

Consider the following strategies for fostering growth and self-improvement on your leadership journey:

Set Personal and Professional Goals:
Establish clear, measurable goals for your personal and professional growth, and regularly assess your progress towards these goals. By setting specific targets, you can maintain focus and motivation on your path towards becoming an unshakable leader.

Engage in Lifelong Learning:
Continuously seek opportunities to expand your knowledge and skills through formal education, professional development courses, workshops, conferences, and self-directed learning. Staying

informed and up-to-date on the latest trends, research, and best practices in leadership can help you stay ahead of the curve and remain effective in a rapidly changing world.

Cultivate a Growth Mindset:
Embrace a growth mindset by viewing challenges and setbacks as opportunities for learning and growth rather than obstacles or failures. This mindset can help you build resilience, perseverance, and adaptability, which are essential qualities for unshakable leaders.

Seek Mentorship and Support:
Surround yourself with mentors, peers, and advisors who can provide guidance, encouragement, and feedback as you navigate your leadership journey. Building a strong support network can help you stay grounded, gain new perspectives, and remain accountable to your growth and self-improvement goals.

Practice Regular Reflection and Self-Assessment:
Take the time to regularly reflect on your experiences, successes, and challenges as a leader. Engage in self-assessment activities to identify patterns, areas for improvement, and opportunities for growth. This practice can help you stay focused, self-aware, and committed to your personal and professional development.

Share Your Knowledge and Experience:
As you grow and develop as a leader, look

for opportunities to share your knowledge and experience with others. Whether through mentoring, teaching, or engaging in community initiatives, sharing your insights and expertise can help you solidify your own learning and contribute to the growth of others.

Embrace Change and Uncertainty:
In today's rapidly changing and unpredictable world, the ability to adapt and embrace uncertainty is a crucial skill for unshakable leaders. Cultivate a mindset of flexibility, curiosity, and openness to change, and view uncertainty as an opportunity for growth and innovation.

Becoming an unshakable leader requires a commitment to embracing your unique leadership style and pursuing continuous growth and self-improvement. By incorporating the unorthodox leadership approaches discussed in this book, you can create a powerful, authentic, and adaptable leadership presence that inspires your team to achieve their full potential.

As you continue on your leadership journey, remember that the path to unshakable leadership is not linear, and you will inevitably encounter challenges, setbacks, and opportunities for growth along the way.

Stay curious, open-minded, and resilient, and embrace the journey as an opportunity to learn, evolve, and make a lasting impact on the world around you.

WANT MORE?

We don't want this book to be an extended sales letter – but at www.motivatrz.com you find more blog posts and online courses helping you to implement those principles even more in your work.

Sign up for the newsletter here and get more inspiration and tips.

Also, remember to connect with us on social where we spill some occasional unorthodox beans:

LINKEDIN

FACEBOOK